Praise

'*Become a Super Salesforce Consultant* presents an exceptionally comprehensive and meticulously crafted roadmap to strategically plan and prepare for a successful journey in the realm of Salesforce.

It is enriched with a wealth of personal anecdotes from the esteemed author and accounts of other individuals who have embarked on similar professional odysseys. As readers immerse themselves in these narratives, they will undoubtedly find resonance and amusement, discovering that they are not alone in their own journey. Delving into each chapter, readers will be instilled with a newfound sense of assurance, empowering them to carve out their own distinct and purposeful career path within the dynamic landscape of Salesforce.'

— **Megan Tuano,** Salesforce Consultant, project manager and Salesforce blogger, www.SalesforcewithMegan.com

'*Become a Super Salesforce Consultant* is a comprehensive resource that will guide you through the process of digital transformation from A to Z, whatever your role. Guidance is provided with a healthy dose of humour and real-world experience, weaving together what to do and, more importantly, what not to do – as well as the potential

consequences. A very fun and informative read for all Salesforce professionals.'
> — **Christine Marshall,** Salesforce MVP and courses and community director at Salesforce Ben

'A great book to refer to regularly as it sets out a useful roadmap of how to approach each project. As a Salesforce newbie, I found it to be an informative and interesting read. It explains things in great detail but its informal approach makes one feel that you don't have to be super techy to read and understand its content.'
> — **Lynn Walker,** Salesforce newbie and Supermums alumnus

'I really enjoyed this book. As a Salesforce project manager, it has helped me to identify risks and I think the detail on what the mitigation options are is particularly valuable. It's jam-packed with great ideas and is a helpful resource to dip in and out of as you need the relevant parts depending on the challenges at hand.'
> — **Liz Whiting,** senior Salesforce project manager

'Following a recent promotion from admin to a consultant job role, *Become a Super Salesforce Consultant* has given me enough information to reflect on my current practice as a consultant and look at the areas I need to invest more time in

developing. I liked the real-life examples used from Heather's experience and the experiences of others. I look forward to applying the learning in practice.'
— **Kate Morris,** Salesforce associate consultant and Supermums alumnus

Heather Black

BECOME A SUPER SALESFORCE CONSULTANT

Superpower your career with this A-to-Z guide on how to lead a Salesforce project

Rethink

First published in Great Britain in 2023 by Rethink Press (www.rethinkpress.com)

© Copyright Heather Black

All rights reserved. No part of this publication may be reproduced, stored in or introduced into a retrieval system, or transmitted, in any form, or by any means (electronic, mechanical, photocopying, recording or otherwise) without the prior written permission of the publisher.

The right of Heather Black to be identified as the author of this work has been asserted by her in accordance with the Copyright, Designs and Patents Act 1988.

This book is sold subject to the condition that it shall not, by way of trade or otherwise, be lent, resold, hired out, or otherwise circulated without the publisher's prior consent in any form of binding or cover other than that in which it is published and without a similar condition including this condition being imposed on the subsequent purchaser.

Contents

Foreword	1
Introduction	3
PART ONE The Role of a Salesforce Consultant	11
1 The Role Of A Salesforce Consultant	13
2 The Benefits Of The Role	21
3 Is Salesforce Consultancy The Right Career For You?	29
PART TWO The Hat-Trick of Consultancy Skills	35
A Agile Project Management	37
B Business Analysis	51

C	Change Management	67
D	DevOps	77

PART THREE   Forming a Team — 87

E	Evaluating The Opportunity	89
F	Four Roles Of An Awesome Admin	97
G	Governance	105
H	Hiring A Team	117
I	Identify And Upskill Salesforce Champions	125
J	Job Roles And Responsibilities	133

PART FOUR   Evaluating the Business Need — 139

K	KPIs For Measuring ROI	141
L	Legacy Adoption Issues	149
M	Mentoring	157
N	Navigating Stakeholders	165
O	Org Analysis	171
P	Project Tools	179

PART FIVE   Preparing for Roll-Out — 185

Q	Quality Testing	187
R	Running A Great Product Demo	197

S Selling Salesforce	205
T Training	213

PART SIX   Embedding Salesforce   221

U User Adoption	223
V Value Assessment	237
W Wrapping Up	241

PART SEVEN   Becoming a Super Consultant   245

X X-Ray Of The Project	247
Y Your Career Plan	251
Z Zone Of Genius	259

Conclusion	263
Acknowledgements	267
Introducing Supermums	269
The Author	273

Foreword

This A to Z guide on how to *Become a Super Salesforce Consultant* provides a fantastic methodology to bring our customers into the digital transformation process from start to finish.

Implementing Salesforce is about connectivity – people sit at the heart of any successful Salesforce implementation. Salesforce consultants need to lead people through the digital transformation with a clear structure, process and the tools to educate, engage and empower them to maximise user adoption and the return on investment for the business.

If you want to excel as a Salesforce professional and confidently lead stakeholders through a Salesforce project to maximise its impact, then this book is for you.

Zahra Bahrololoumi CBE
CEO UK/I Salesforce

Introduction

Would you like a structure and process for leading people through the digital transformation of your Salesforce project from planning through to roll-out? Do you want to know how to engage, enthuse and empower your stakeholders to maximise user adoption and return on investment (ROI)?

If yes, then this book is for you. It provides a step-by-step process with handy tools and templates to enable you to lead all your stakeholders, from C-suite to front-line staff, confidently through a project to ensure trust and assurance.

In this book I walk you through the project life cycle from A to Z with a focus on how to connect with the people in the project. In it, we will cover:

- The role of a Salesforce consultant
- Core consultancy skills
- How to establish a team
- How to evaluate the business need
- How to communicate with stakeholders
- How to prepare for roll-out
- How to embed the system
- How to evaluate project success
- How to establish and accelerate your career

If you have the title of executive sponsor, Salesforce admin, product manager, or Salesforce consultant, you are likely to hold the responsibility for taking people on a journey of digital transformation. With this responsibility, you are in essence the in-house or external Salesforce consultant and your users are your client; I want you to own this role and so will empower you through the use of this terminology throughout the book. Whether you are working in-house or externally, you need to present yourself in a professional way – applying disciplines, methodology and processes to the way you work as a Salesforce consultant. As Salesforce professionals, we specialise in helping our clients to adopt processes and systems, so we need to apply the same rigour in our approach to consulting. If you want to land a role with this level of professional autonomy and do well, then you need

INTRODUCTION

to have the hat-trick of consultancy skills – the content within this book will give you a good boost in the right direction.

Capacity to deploy this process isn't about having years of technical experience, but rather about knowing and applying the methodologies of business analysis, Agile project management and change management, in a considered way. You can learn and apply these disciplines from day one to boost your credibility, experience and capability. Being equipped with these skills will super-charge your Salesforce career in terms of your confidence, skills, knowledge and salary.

I have witnessed first-hand how learning these principles has multiplied an individual's career opportunities within the Salesforce ecosystem. I love seeing the journeys of the trainees who participate in the Supermums Consultancy Skills course I deliver. Here are just some of the success stories:

- Shenita relaunched her career as a virtual freelance Salesforce consultant.
- Margaret stood out at interview with the skills and templates to land her first role.
- Ben professionalised his skills and landed a promotion from admin to functional architect.
- Candy developed an implementation plan for her product manager role.

- Jennifer gained confidence in her new Salesforce consultancy role.
- Julianne was able to ask the right questions to prospective clients in her pre-sales role.
- Sherrian was able to lead a Salesforce project as a solo Salesforce admin.

It's time to get focused on your success. Avoid getting it wrong by finding out how to get it right – you can read this book in just four hours and accelerate your confidence and career.

My inspiration for writing this book came from eleven years of working as a Salesforce consultant, ten years running an award-winning Salesforce consultancy and, for the last three years, more specifically training and advising executive sponsors and Salesforce professionals on consultancy skills and how to lead projects. I have overseen over 700 projects with 350 customers, and I've witnessed why things go wrong versus why they go right.

When a project goes wrong, it isn't pleasant. It often involves difficult conversations, overtime (which could be unpaid if you're a freelancer), stress, unwanted pressures, and, depending on the nature of the problem, it could result in delays to the go-live of the system and impact end-user adoption, with financial ramifications for the organisation. None of these things you want to be responsible for or experience,

INTRODUCTION

and, in most cases, they can be easily avoided if you learn how.

I catalogued all of the problems I'd seen on projects and came up with twenty risks, which I put into a risk assessment template. You should educate your client about these risks upfront and mitigate as many as possible by upskilling yourself and, more importantly, equipping your client with the resources they need.

When I started out as a consultant, I thought I knew what I was doing. I had trained in admin, advanced admin and had also done a consultancy skills course with Salesforce that focused mostly on the design of the system – but I still didn't know how to apply a professional approach to business analysis, Agile project management and change management. As a freelance consultant with no background in tech projects, I quickly realised I didn't know how to manage a project properly. I didn't know how to document things in the right way. I didn't know how to get stakeholders engaged if they were resisting Salesforce. I didn't know how to prioritise requirements if the client had more things on their wish list than they had budget for. There were many other things I didn't know.

I was just making it up as I went, and that didn't feel good. I felt like an imposter and out of my depth. So I researched what qualifications other Salesforce consultants had and decided to invest over £10k in a series of professional training courses, including the

Agile Project Management Group (APMG) Change Management and Agile Project Management Foundation certifications and the BCS Business Analysis Diploma to complement the NLP practitioner training I already had. I was confident the investment would pay off, not only in terms of confidence but also in terms of my professionalism, ability to win projects and earning potential.

From starting out as a freelance Salesforce consultant working three days a week and earning £60k a year in 2012, I grew a Salesforce consultancy to twenty people and had worked on over 700 projects by 2021. We won the EMEA Salesforce Partner of the Year Award, had a 65% repeat/referral customer rate and 4.5/5 rating on the Salesforce AppExchange. The professional skills and methodologies that we applied to projects were what secured us this reputation. There is a recipe for this success, and I created a series of templates and tools to enable my team of consultants to apply a consistent approach to all projects.

I now focus my time on training and advising executive sponsors, Centre of Excellence (CoE) teams and Salesforce professionals, either privately or through the Supermums Consultancy Skills course, sharing all of the great content I have learnt about and curated over the years.

At Supermums, we love launching and boosting the careers of new and existing Salesforce professionals through our training courses and recruitment services. Our non-profit mission is to support more women into tech, but our services are open to anyone. To learn more about Supermums and to download a heap of free resources and templates, look to the resource page for this book on our website.

Much of the advice shared in this book is taken from content in my Supermums Consultancy Skills course and our weekly Career Boost News Bulletin. Find out more at www.supermums.org.

PART ONE
THE ROLE OF A SALESFORCE CONSULTANT

1
The Role Of A Salesforce Consultant

What do you believe your role as a Salesforce consultant to be? What is the ideal – and what is the reality?

In this chapter, I talk through my own career story. I get real, as I walk you through the ideal of making people happy but also the realities of the challenges you can face. Ride the highs and the lows with me as we carve out your vision and talk through the roles and responsibilities of a Salesforce consultant.

When you have learnt the basics of the role, then you can plan for the future. For example, in Chapters Y and Z I will help you to see how you can double your salary as a Salesforce professional, starting at the bottom and working your way up. It's possible to achieve all your ambitions by investing time in learning and development. But first, getting a clear vision for your career will give you the motivation for investing that time. You are only going to invest time in reading this book if you have a clear vision and are motivated to boost your career and develop the superpowers to achieve it, so let's figure out what that is.

My story

It may help you identify your vision if I tell you a little bit about mine. I became an accidental admin for a non-profit I was running back in 2010. I had sat with the free Salesforce licences for a couple of years, but I really had no idea of what Salesforce could do for me. It was only when another non-profit gave me a demo of how they used Salesforce that the lightbulb moment happened – that was it, I was sold. I was so excited about the future and I couldn't wait to get started. Take note that it was this demo that made all the difference; seeing what was possible engaged and excited me about using it.

I enrolled onto the admin course, and I decided to build my own Salesforce system. I thought that surely I could do it myself – why would I need help? It was only a few weeks later that I also enrolled onto the Salesforce 'Consultancy Skills' course (sadly no longer available), and I learnt how to gather requirements and design, rather than build, a system. Low and behold, I had to completely rebuild my Salesforce system from scratch so that I could actually produce the reports and dashboards that I wanted, amongst other things. I share more about my top ten rookie mistakes later, which I'm sure will resonate with many of you. Thankfully, I hadn't yet gone live with my Salesforce system with my end users. If I had, there might have been some bigger issues to resolve related to data, training and user adoption.

Once I got the model right, Salesforce was the living, beating heart of my business and it boosted my earning potential. I was able to extract valuable performance data from the system that enabled me to win more work, and I scaled my non-profit from £100k to £1.3m in a year. It was a rollercoaster of a ride as we went from four staff to forty, and I couldn't have achieved or supported this growth without the capabilities of Salesforce. I was so impressed with how it could support my non-profit to manage all of the different aspects of the business, including my employees, that I decided I wanted to help other non-profits harness the power of Salesforce too. This whet my appetite to become a Salesforce consultant and to help other non-profits achieve growth.

When I decided to pursue this path, I was just thirty-three – what did I think I was getting into, and why did I believe I could do it?

Let's start with the job. I imagined it would involve:

- Talking through and redefining processes with teams
- Identifying what goals and indicators would define performance
- Understanding how technology could better enhance a team's performance and well-being
- Figuring out and implementing technology solutions to meet the client's needs

I believed I could do this because:

- I had completed the Admin, Advanced Admin and Consultancy Skills Salesforce courses (the latter they no longer teach, but I cover the content in the Supermums Consultancy Skills course)
- I had worked as a hands-on Salesforce admin on my own Salesforce system for two years
- I had run a business and was a qualified business coach. I had coached entrepreneurs for several years, asking them questions to improve their processes, strategies and goals

I decided to focus on working with other non-profits, as it was a sector I knew well and felt passionate about, having run a non-profit myself for seven years and supported others doing the same previously.

I then investigated what new skills I might need to learn by looking at other people's credentials and decided I would need to invest in further training to help me upskill.

There were a few things I felt unsure about in my early days as a Salesforce consultant. First, how to gather document requirements in the 'proper' way to share with stakeholders. This led me to learn about formal business analysis skills. I had not heard of this term before, but I invested in a four-week course and I was blown away. I loved it. Much of it felt familiar, due to my business coaching background, but it gave me the tools, methodology and templates to gather requirements and document things properly, rather than just ask random questions.

Second, I was unsure how to manage Customer Relationship Management (CRM) and digital transformation projects properly. It was clear to see early on that the 'wish list' of requirements from clients was not well-defined upfront, so how I could estimate a cost for implementation? Alternatively, it would be immediately obvious that their budget would not cover everything that they had identified during the business analysis stage – how would I deal with this? You want to please clients, so it felt uncomfortable telling them that they could not have everything they wanted for their budget. I needed to know how to manage this situation. This is when I learnt about Agile DSDM (the Dynamic System Development Method) project management. This is the commonly used method of agreeing a time and budget but being flexible on requirements, which is the norm for technical projects. It gave me the project management framework I needed to manage clients successfully.

The next thing I needed to get my head around was how best to facilitate negative reactions to a CRM system. I lived in my happy place, where everyone understood how wonderful Salesforce was, and would start the engagement with the executive sponsor who would be equally enthused about the changes to come. But when you get to meet the rest of the team, there are often a mix of different emotions and attitudes towards the pending new CRM, from anger to fear, upset, resentment and excitement. How do you facilitate a group of managers and staff with so much mixed energy in the room? As a Salesforce consultant, people look to you for reassurance and trust that the system will deliver. I wanted to know how to facilitate this change process in a positive and inspiring way, so I decided to do a course in change management. I realised that CRM projects were largely about guiding people on a journey of change. Only if you got this people engagement process right would you achieve the digital transformation that you were striving for. This change management course, alongside my coaching skills, gave me the knowledge and skills to deploy people strategies aligned to the culture of the organisation.

I also needed to know how to set clients up for success beyond my engagement as a consultant. I wanted clients to adopt the system and take ownership of it beyond my help, but how could I achieve this? I realised that there needed to be a risk appraisal at the outset to help clients understand the risks and help them mitigate these through a set of interventions. A simple example being, who would be their appointed Salesforce admin(s)? What training could they do to feel better equipped? And how could I get them engaged in the Salesforce Ohana and Trailhead? A common pitfall is that no one takes up the mantel. I now have over twenty risks in my risk register and, sadly, a few clients where Salesforce was implemented but never adopted as some of these risks weren't mitigated.

Navigating the road to success

When you are equipped to handle the different challenges that might arise, you can feel empowered to deliver as a consultant. Otherwise, it can be stressful, intimidating and overwhelming. At the end of the day, a business is entrusting you with making a major change to how they work.

The consultancy role was what I imagined it to be, but it required confidence in myself and a careful orchestration of skills and capabilities to achieve the right results. When I started out, I was in my early thirties and quite often found myself consulting with a team of managers much older than me. I had to work hard to demonstrate my capacity and skills to convince them that I could deliver and to gain their trust.

It's important to know that you will not get it right all the time. You will learn something new from every project you do, so reflect and do things differently next time by deploying new strategies and learning new techniques. For this reason, I include reflection activities and next steps in Chapters X and Z.

As a successful Salesforce consultant, you will be rewarded by:

- Transforming how an organisation uses digital tools to make it more efficient and profitable.
- Making business owners and teams much happier in their job roles.
- Helping people enter the wonderful world of the Salesforce Ohana.

It is a great job if you set yourself up for success. This book helps you do just that.

2
The Benefits Of The Role

A Salesforce career will make you happy, because it is about making other people happy – and that is the best feeling in the world.

Whenever I started a new Salesforce project with a client, my opening message would be: 'My ultimate goal is to make you happy and ensure you have a smile on your face by the time I finish this project, and this is why.'

Then I would talk about the following points, to gain their trust and buy-in. You can use these as ideas for your opening conversations with clients.

'As a Salesforce professional, I want to…'

- **Help you solve your pain points.** I want to know about the things that frustrate you about your current system or way of working. Treat our workshops as counselling sessions, where you can share frustrations as we talk through these processes and I will share with you what's possible, and we'll work together to find solutions.

- **Help take boring administration from your desk** so we can focus your time on the things that excite you the most. We reduce admin through automating processes, for example sending emails automatically, or getting clients to input their information in the system through online forms. Together, let's see how much time we can save you, so you have less admin, finish work on time and can spend more time doing the things you love.

- **Help you achieve and exceed your performance targets** by improving your working processes and the overall customer experience. Tell me what would help you to make a shift towards producing better outcomes for your customers. What do you need that will help you deliver a better service for your prospects and clients?

- **Help you sleep better at night and relax on holiday.** With Salesforce, you have Big Brother level visibility of performance and information at the touch of the button. You don't need to ask and wait to understand how things are going; you can watch from a distance and know that things are happening.

- **Help the business leaders achieve their business goals.** How? Through implementing a solution that everyone enjoys using and, in return, improves the efficiency and performance of their team and so increases customer satisfaction and retention.

- **Spend time getting under the hood of your business.** I want to understand what makes things tick and design a solution that is going to work for all team members. Ultimately, Salesforce should become the beating heart of your business, something that everyone wants to use every day as they can't live without it.

- **Coach you to feel empowered with new technology.** I am excited to introduce you to Salesforce, the number one CRM system globally, and to open your eyes to what's possible. I want to coach and empower you to use new technology that will be customised to meet your needs.

- **Add value to your project.** I can add value to this project because of my experience in your industry, with the technology and with similar processes. These are some of the great outcomes I have achieved for similar clients – I'm looking forward to helping you to achieve similar.

Finally, I would close by saying something like: 'Ultimately, I want to see a smile on your face when I leave you with a new system – then I will know it's a job well done.'

Personally, I enjoy helping businesses to streamline their processes, clean up their data, see their performance more clearly and analyse what they can do better. In essence, a Salesforce professional is also a management consultant. You can help them to change the way they manage their business for the better, through the power of technology. It's a fantastic feeling to see how you have transformed a business and to reflect on the journey from where they were to where they are one year on.

The reality if you don't get it right

The ideal world of making people happy only happens if you avoid mistakes. But you don't know what you don't know, and it's easy to make mistakes if you haven't yet built the skills and learnt the tricks of the trade. As a helping hand, below I've listed what I consider the ten rookie mistakes; you can avoid these by learning and applying the A to Z methodology I provide in this book.

1. **Not preparing the business case to generate buy-in for the implementation.** Senior managers will ask: 'Why should I spend this money? What will the benefits be? How will it help me save

money, make money, reduce wastage or retain staff?' You will fail to engage stakeholders in the project if there isn't a clear business case. A consultant needs to work with the client to produce and communicate tangible business benefits. Check out Chapter B to learn more about the business case and what documentation to produce for your Salesforce project.

2. **Not onboarding Salesforce customers properly.** Not having an onboarding checklist can result in significant delays in a project. I recommend a ten-step onboarding process that includes steps such as accessing their system, risk analysis, nominated internal admins and more. Check out Chapter F to understand how to get the foundations in place for a high-performing team.

3. **Not appraising and mitigating risks.** Avoid possible risks by identifying and discussing them with the client so they can be mitigated upfront. In Chapter G we will run through some common risks.

4. **Not briefing a client ahead of their Salesforce design workshop.** You could waste valuable time and budget on a design workshop if people show up unprepared. A good consultant should present the process and distribute questionnaires in advance of the workshop so people come armed with the information they need. In Chapter B we'll learn how to prepare a client for business analysis.

5. **Not asking the right questions in the design workshops.** There are so many questions you need to ask that it's impossible to come up with them on the spot or remember them in your head each time you start a project. A consultant should have ready-prepared presentations and questions for different Salesforce products to cover everything. This is part of the business analysis, which we discuss in Chapter B.

6. **Not making time for conversations to capture the non-functional requirements.** Leaving out non-functional requirements can leave a system open to security and compliance issues if these areas haven't been discussed. Quite often, all of the time and emphasis is given to functional requirements – leave some budget available for non-functional things too.

7. **Not documenting agreed requirements.** Not having a shared document detailing what was discussed and agreed between all parties is never going to end well, as it's difficult to demonstrate agreement on prioritisation and deliverables. A consultant should document all discussions through process maps, a requirements log, technical workbook and more. In Chapter B, we'll run through what documentation you need – I'll also provide a couple of free templates .

8. **Not engaging people properly in the project.** Are you communicating in the right way to

grab people's attention? It's the consultant's responsibility to plan a communication strategy that will enthuse, engage and empower stakeholders. Within Chapters C and N we'll talk through a change management strategy and learn how to communicate with different types of stakeholders.

9. **Not training people properly on how to use the system.** If users don't understand how to use the system, you might be training them in the wrong way. A training strategy needs to sell the value of Salesforce as well as explain how to use it. It's important to deliver training in ways that suit different learning styles and motivate people to engage. Within Chapters S and T we will learn how to use training strategies to boost user adoption.

10. **Not helping the customer to set up a Centre of Excellence.** Leaving a customer with a Salesforce org without a CoE is like leaving a baby without a parent to look after it. It's going to get into trouble. A CoE embeds a governance structure to manage the CRM long term. A consultant should advise on the roles and responsibilities of the executive sponsor, management team, Salesforce admins and Salesforce champions. In Chapter G, we run through what is needed and how to put this governance in place.

3
Is Salesforce Consultancy The Right Career For You?

What are Salesforce consultants, and what do they do?

A Salesforce consultant typically wears multiple hats. They might work in-house within a company or be contracted as an external consultant to help a business get the most out of their Salesforce CRM. They conduct business analysis with a client to understand their business goals and processes, their pain points and the opportunities for technology to support them. They also have the technical knowledge to design and/or implement solutions to enhance the business processes and performance. They are in a trusted position of authority, hired to help transform the way a team works in order to improve customer service and organisational performance. A good consultant understands the platform but also has good business analysis, project management and change management skills to guide people and organisations through the process of solving critical business problems.

More and more companies are turning to tools such as Salesforce CRM to streamline the process of managing client relations, but not all businesspeople are savvy in their use of the latest software. That is where the role of the Salesforce consultant comes in.

Some of the responsibilities of a Salesforce consultant include:

- Managing the client relationship
- Creating and managing project plans
- Mapping out business processes
- Supporting people through change
- Gathering functional (business) requirements
- Managing a team of technical staff
- Proposing technical requirements
- Technical product configuration
- User testing and training

The Salesforce consultant helps businesses to get the most out of their Salesforce platform. Their knowledge of both the platform and business practices combined with excellent communication skills, makes them a valuable asset to any company and it's why they are rewarded with an excellent salary.

Experience and certifications

If you are interested in becoming a Salesforce consultant, one of the first things to consider is the qualifications and experience needed. Once of the main assets is business experience. Typically, customers want to hire consultants who have a background in an industry relevant to their own, as they will be able to understand their terminology, resonate with their pain points, speak their language, know the KPIs and build trust much more quickly. You won't need to learn the industry jargon and can quickly add value to their process. Salesforce typically sells into specific industry verticals, namely media, retail, marketing, sales, automotive, consumer goods, education, communication, energy and utilities, financial services, healthcare and life sciences, manufacturing, public sector, non-profit, and technology, as well as horizontals such as sales, service and marketing. You may find that the experience you have gained in previous roles can help you on your way to becoming a Salesforce consultant.

The next thing to consider is platform knowledge and certifications. If you are already a Salesforce admin, you will more than likely have at least two certifications (Salesforce Admin and then Platform App Builder are great starting points) but the longer you have worked with Salesforce, the more likely you are to secure those higher-paid roles, especially if you add a Salesforce consultant certification to your CV or résumé. Start with a product that you feel experienced in; for example, if you have a background in sales, pursue the Sales Cloud Consultant Certification; if you have a background in customer service, pursue the Service Cloud Consultant Certification, and so on.

But if you plan to take responsibility for gathering requirements, engaging stakeholders in digital transformation and managing a Salesforce implementation professionally, then you will need an additional skill set beyond the standard Salesforce certifications.

Skills that every Salesforce solo admin or consultant should possess include:

- Agile project management
- Business analysis
- Change management
- DevOps

At the start of your journey with this book, I recommend that you take our Consultancy Skills Benchmark Quiz to assess your baseline level of knowledge. This can be found on the book resources page here.

Now let's get started with the A to Z. Chapters A to D provide an introduction to the core professional disciplines; then in Chapters E to Z we delve into how these core disciplines integrate with different activities throughout the project life cycle.

PART TWO
THE HAT-TRICK OF CONSULTANCY SKILLS

A
Agile Project Management

> You customer demands, 'What do you mean I can't have all of the requirements?'
>
> *As a consultant, do you know how to say 'no' to customers and manage scope creep?*

In this chapter, we'll find out how to prioritise requirements within time and budget by learning more about Agile project management (PM).

Have you ever been in the situation where you have a list of requirements as long as your arm, but the client just doesn't have the budget? You either did such a great job getting them excited about Salesforce that they now have an overflowing wish list, or you discovered that their processes have lots of intricacies that you never imagined. How do you manage the expectations of the client and get them to prioritise without it being an awkward conversation?

If the client hasn't bought into a clear methodology for prioritising requirements within an agreed time and budget, then everything will be a bit unclear and unstructured and quite often they will expect to get everything on their wish list, leaving you swallowing the time as you can't say no. This is where Agile Dynamic System Development Method (DSDM) project management fits in.

WHAT CAN GO WRONG?

Below are three different challenging scenarios that can arise on projects when Agile DSDM project management isn't properly embedded.

1. The Salesforce team proceed to build the list of requirements without asking the client to prioritise them. The team run out of budget before they have incorporated all of the requirements and inform the client that they can't do any more. The client is not happy that they haven't been asked which requirements to prioritise, as they would have chosen to build other requirements first. As a result, the team has to finish the other requirements at their own cost. What should have happened? The Salesforce team should have checked in with the client on a weekly basis about what to prioritise, to give the client control over the budget and deliverables.

2. There are three different department managers on the client side, all discussing and prioritising their requirements with the Salesforce team, but there is one overall budget pot. The Salesforce team are delivering on these different requirements but once

all of the budget is utilised it becomes apparent that the client is expecting all of their requirements to be met. Two things have gone wrong here. First, there should have been a client-side project manager triaging and prioritising all of the requirements across the three departments to maximise use of budget. Second, the client wasn't wholly bought into the Agile PM methodology, despite it being discussed at the pitch and onboarding session. There should have been a more formal 'training' session on Agile methodology with the client team to make sure they were all bought into the process.

3. Within a design workshop, the individuals don't understand why their requirements aren't being prioritised and start to get disengaged and frustrated. This situation can arise if the Agile PM is explained to the executive team but not to the individuals participating in the design workshops. In ideal circumstances, the Salesforce team should prepare all the stakeholders by delivering a training session on Agile DSDM project management with anyone involved in the design process.

HOW TO GET IT RIGHT

It's important to understand and get trained up in Agile DSDM project management so you feel confident delivering this methodology on a project.

Within this chapter you will learn more about Agile PM, why it's important, what it's value is and why it is the norm for tech agencies. You'll also get clear on the difference between traditional project management versus Agile PM methodologies, and which Agile methodology would best suit your job role.

What is Agile PM?

Agile PM evolved in the '90s with a specific focus on technology projects; since then, organisations large and small have embraced the new age of Agile.

There are four key things to understand about Agile PM:

1. 'Agile project management' is an umbrella term for a variety of different methods – the Dynamic Systems Development Method (DSDM), Scrum and Lean are some examples.
2. Agile focuses on prioritisation and iteration of flexible requirements, working within time and budget constraints using MoSCoW prioritisation.
3. Agile is now considered the norm for technology projects.
4. Agile is a global project management practice, with tools and systems to manage requirements, time and costs.

Why is Agile PM important and valuable?

If there's a long wish list of requirements and demands with no prioritisation or project management, you will find it a challenge to meet the expectations of clients and teams. This can lead to frustration on all sides, and will result in:

- Requirements not being correctly prioritised and budget spent in the wrong areas
- Half-baked solutions
- Technology not aligning to business need
- Overspend on budget
- Timeframes not being met

Organisations are increasingly embracing Agile as a technique for managing projects. A recent global survey found that 71% of organisations report using Agile approaches for their projects sometimes, often or always.[1] A report by APMG showed that the greater the utilisation of Agile methods in a project, the more successful that project is in meeting all its aims.[2]

---

1 PMI *Pulse of the Profession: 9th Global Project Management Survey* (PMI, 2017) www.pmi.org/-/media/pmi/documents/public/pdf/learning/thought-leadership/pulse/pulse-of-the-profession-2017.pdf

2 P Serrador and JK Pinto, 'Does Agile work? A quantitative analysis of Agile project success', *International Journal of Project Management*, 33/5(2015), 1040–1051, www.apm.org.uk/media/7550/does-agile-work-a-quantitative-analysis-of-agile-project-success.pdf, accessed August 2023

Senior executives increasingly recognise that Agile is 'eating the world'.[3] In fact, surveys by both Deloitte and McKinsey show that over 90% of senior executives want to be agile, while less than 10% currently see their own firm as 'highly agile'. There are now major efforts underway with 'Agile transformations' being planned or implemented in many organisations, both public and private. All the successful software firms are recognisably implementing the substance of Agile – a focus on delivering value for customers, working in small teams in short cycles, and networked organisational arrangements rather than top-down bureaucracy and silos[4].

Why is Agile PM the norm in tech?

This comes down to practicalities. In the context of technology agencies and projects, rarely is there a detailed technical specification designed upfront, so it's usually impossible, or at least high risk, for agencies to give a fixed price on a project when requirements are unknown. Technology is advancing all the time and market conditions are ever-changing, meaning there may be a need to evolve solutions and

---

3   Denning, S, 'Agile Is Not Just Another Management Fad' *Forbes* (30 July 2018), www.forbes.com/sites/stevedenning/2018/07/30/agile-is-not-just-another-management-fad/?sh=571a4ea31957, accessed 4 September 2023
4   Ibid.

requirements as needed throughout the lifetime of the project.

Often, the client doesn't know or understand the technical features available at the outset of the project, so the Agile process provides the user with the flexibility to evolve their requirements throughout the project as they learn more about their approach. Quick wins build confidence, so if you can develop a system in stages this will allow users to see and celebrate success in earlier stages without committing to a whole project.

Typically, there is a fixed budget for a project (with contingency). It is in the best interests of both the client and the consultancy to deliver on high-priority requirements within this budget, without compromising the working relationship or quality. This reduces the risk for both the client and the partner, as they can choose to allocate and spend resources as needed rather than stick rigidly to an upfront plan.

Traditional versus Agile

What is the difference between traditional Waterfall PM compared to Agile PM?

In Waterfall PM:

- Budget and time can escalate for the consultancy or the client, depending on the agreement.

- All requirements that have been agreed upon are to be delivered.
- Requirements are agreed upfront as part of the initial contract.
- There is typically no flexibility throughout the project in changing these requirements.
- The design process is sequential: build, test, roll out for the full project.

By contrast, in Agile DSDM project management:

- Budget and time are fixed and agreed upfront but can be increased.
- Requirements are prioritised throughout and aligned to business need.
- There is an iterative process where design, build, test and roll-out happen throughout.
- Flexibility is key throughout the project life cycle.

Which Agile PM methodology suits your job role?

As mentioned, there are various methods within the umbrella term of 'Agile' PM, but the two main ones are DSDM and Scrum.

DSDM

DSDM is an Agile method that focuses on the full project life cycle.[5] DSDM was developed in 1994, after project managers using RAD (rapid application development) sought more governance and discipline in this new, iterative way of working.

DSDM's success is due to the philosophy that 'any project must be aligned to clearly defined strategic goals and focus upon early delivery of real benefits to the business'.[6] This philosophy is supported by eight principles that allow teams to maintain focus and achieve the project goals.

The eight principles of DSDM:

1. Focus on the business need

2. Deliver on time

3. Collaborate

4. Never compromise quality

5. Build incrementally from firm foundations

6. Develop iteratively

7. Communicate continuously and clearly

8. Demonstrate control

---

5   More information about DSDM can be found at www.agilebusiness.org/dsdm-project-framework.html
6   www.agilebusiness.org/business-agility/what-is-dsdm.html

The DSDM approach is the best methodology if you manage CRM implementations at a strategic level, working with the executive team and managing both the business analysis and technical team. It helps you to see the big picture and prioritise projects and requirements. This would suit a Salesforce project manager or solo Salesforce administrator/system manager.

DSDM may also be used to supplement an existing in-house Agile approach, where this has proved to be lacking. For example, DSDM is often used to provide the full 'project' focus to complement Scrum's team-focused product development process.

Scrum

Scrum is the best methodology if you have been given a sub-set of technical requirements and you are managing a technical team to implement those requirements on a daily basis. This method would best suit a Salesforce technical lead who is managing the daily build of a solution.

How do you estimate a project budget?

Project management is all about delivering projects on time and within budget, and one of the most common questions I get asked is, 'How do I estimate the cost of a project?'

First, you need to decide which PM methodology you are going to use to manage time and budget estimate, Agile or Waterfall. Second, identify how many projects there are – map out how many teams and/or departments need their own processes and requirements analysed.

You can then start to estimate a budget for the whole project life cycle. The budget has to cover the time required for onboarding, design, implement (build), user testing, training, offboarding and project management.

- **Onboarding:** onboarding tasks include project planning, communicating the process, preparation support, acquiring licences and more.

- **Design:** design time includes delivering business analysis (BA) preparation workshops, reviewing BA questionnaires, facilitating design workshops, writing up requirements and researching solutions.

- **Implementation:** this is the effort required for the detailed build of the system and will depend on the number of objects, fields, email templates, flows, security and so on. For this type of estimation, I created a budget calculator that enabled me to plug numbers into a table against deliverables to calculate effort involved. Alternatively, other Agile methods use story points related to effort.

- **User testing:** this includes preparation of sandboxes, test data, demos, user testing scripts and walk-throughs, plus change requests and repeat tests.

- **Training:** this includes preparation of the required training content, which could involve producing a demo, prepping sandboxes, preparing presentations, creating a Trailhead path, setting up in-situ training tools, creating walk-through videos, writing manuals, producing training scripts or delivering live training.

- **Offboarding:** this includes training a Salesforce admin on their roles and responsibilities, setting up a support desk, introducing new admins to the Salesforce Ohana, Trailhead and aftercare.

- **Project management:** this includes time spent on client communication, communication with your Salesforce team if relevant, updating and managing a PM system to log deliverables, tasks and time, and consulting on requirements.

REFLECTIVE EXERCISE

Grab a notebook and write down some thoughts on the questions below. This will identify what steps you need to take to boost your confidence and knowledge about Agile PM.

- How equipped and confident are you with Agile PM skills?

- Do you have presentation templates to train your client/team on Agile PM?
- Do you have roles and responsibilities for a project management team, with a communication plan to manage and agree priorities and sign off?
- Do you feel confident estimating and prioritising requirements, running with sprints/time boxes and managing the delivery of requirements, budget and time?
- Do you have systems and tools to manage projects?

At the end of this chapter, you should have a better understanding of why Agile PM is so valuable, and of the role it plays in managing expectations related to a project and improving the communication with customers on deliverables.

B
Business Analysis

> Your customer asks, 'Why is this CRM useful to me or the business?'
>
> *As the consultant, do you know how uncover the business needs from the strategic to the granular level, and communicate the ROI of a CRM?*

This chapter will explain how to conduct business analysis (BA) with stakeholders and demonstrate the benefits for the business at all levels.

Have you ever been in a situation where someone is trying to make you use something that is of no interest or relevance to you? It doesn't resonate with your needs. No one has asked your opinion. You don't see the value and, quite frankly, you are not interested, but they seem insistent on selling it to you.

This is the situation that arises when you don't conduct proper BA with the stakeholders who are your intended Salesforce users. It leads to huge adoption issues as the product isn't fit for purpose and the end users aren't bought into using it.

WHAT CAN GO WRONG?

Below are three challenging scenarios that can occur on projects when BA hasn't been rigorously applied.

1. An organisation has spent millions on a Salesforce implementation and, two years on, the management has no real understanding of what they have invested in or why, what work has been carried out across departments or the ROI value it is bringing to the organisation. None of the departmental managers understands or uses Salesforce and there is only ad-hoc use by the teams they manage. No business case with clear KPIs was created at the beginning of the project and the in-house Salesforce team and external consultants haven't been consistent in recording the work delivered, so there is a lack of detail about what budget/time has been spent on and by whom. The C-suite halt all investment and ask for a full evaluation to try and unpack everything that has been done and what value it offers and are threatening to pull the plug.

2. You walk into a design workshop where none of the users are particularly engaged. This is a problem that often arises when the executive sponsor hasn't done their bit in communicating the business case and getting people's buy-in to the proposed new system. You will never get a system implemented if the people attending your design workshops haven't

prepared the necessary information. If you have resisters, you have a problem. The project will never go live. You need to consult with the executive sponsor about what they communicate and when in order to get people onboard.

3. A new project manager and Salesforce admin are appointed towards the end of a project. The new stakeholders want clarity about what things have been implemented, how and why, but this information hasn't been documented and so isn't available. The new staff members waste weeks trying to work out what has been done and what still needs doing, and the go-live date is missed. When there is no audit trail on a project it can became a source of conflict. Documenting who has asked for what requirements and why, is crucial, especially where there are staff changes.

HOW TO GET IT RIGHT

It is important to understand and sell how the CRM is going to help the users personally as well as how it will help the business, so that everyone is clear on the business value and priorities of the project.

In this section, you will learn how to conduct a thorough BA that will help you gather business requirements in a professional way. This will also enable you to build the trust of your clients and deliver a solution that achieves the desired business outcomes.

Introduction to business analysis

In a LinkedIn poll we posted, 43% voted poor BA as the biggest risk to Salesforce projects,[7] and this concern is echoed within industry reports.

Recent research has found that, on average, performance virtually doubled as organisations progressed from using an ad-hoc approach for requirements definition and management to having institutionalised and consistent competency in all capability areas. The research highlighted the following stats:[8]

- Average on-time performance of technology projects increased by 161%
- Time overruns on projects reduced by 87%
- Average on-budget performance for technology projects improved by just over 95%
- Budget overruns reduced by just under 75%
- Percentage of projects that deliver the functionality needed by the business rose by just over 75%

---

7 www.linkedin.com/posts/heather-black-salesforce-women-in-tech-speaker_salesforce-activity-7046012463007285248-0EYJ?utm_source=share&utm_medium=member_desktop, accessed 4 September 2023
8 IAG Consulting, 'Business Analysis Benchmark – Full Report', www.iag.biz/resource/business-analysis-benchmark-full-report, accessed 4 September 2023

- Average functionality missed dropped by approximately 78%

BA isn't a standalone discipline, however; it must be interwoven with Agile PM and change management skills to be fully effective. This is because, when the BA workshops uncover hundreds of requirements, you need to know how to prioritise these, with the input of the client, using Agile DSDM project management. This prioritisation requires that you know the most pressing business priorities and ROI expectations so that you can align with these.

The stakeholders also need to be engaged, enthused and empowered during the BA process. Adopting appropriate change management techniques during BA elicitation is key to generating buy-in during the design period and training workshops.

What is a business analyst?

Within the Salesforce world, a business analyst is someone who analyses a business process, identifies the pain points and helps the client to prioritise areas that can be improved using technology.

Business analyst techniques are great skills to have in any Salesforce-related job role, whether it's sales, admin, consultant, architect – or straight business analyst, of course. Why? Because technology will only be successful if it is solving a business need and helps the company, team or individual to perform better.

In order for a technology transformation project to be successful, it is imperative that:

- Processes are reviewed in detail and improved
- Priorities are scrutinised and agreed
- Technology options are appraised
- Goals and outcomes are measurable and clear

The four principles of BA are summarised in the POPIT decision-making model:

POPIT model

- **People:** you need to assess the skills and needs of the stakeholders involved – what are their needs, pain points and aspirations?

- **Organisation:** you also need to assess the business, its strategy, its culture and what it is striving to achieve.

- **Processes:** assess the current state of the processes and determine the aspirations for improving and refining these processes to meet the needs of the people and the organisation.

- **Information and Technology:** assess the current technology use and identify future possible needs based on the people, organisation and processes to determine the best solutions to meet those needs.

Agreeing the CRM strategy

Ghada Fourane, former director at Slalom, helpfully summarises the importance of producing a CRM strategy, or roadmap, that outlines the BA discussions with the senior executive team at project kick-off. It's the first stage of the BA process before you dive into detailed analysis with specific teams and departments. Ghada says:

> 'A roadmap is a strategic plan that defines a goal or the desired outcome, which includes the major steps or milestones needed to reach it. It is also great to use as a communication

tool, as it serves as a high-level document that helps articulate strategic thinking – the why – behind both the goal and the plan for getting there to stakeholders.'[9]

The CRM roadmap is defined by strategic goals, which are then prioritised by the Salesforce consultant who can look to see what component of the platform is best suited to cater for that strategy and what the timeframe/order of implementation will be. It should map out the CRM roll-out across and between departments, and the implementation of different Salesforce and independent software vendor (ISV) products, to deliver on the desired business objectives and priorities.

It is important to have a CRM roadmap because, if there aren't clear priorities, the CoE and Salesforce delivery team won't have a North Star to focus on. They won't know what to work on first to best improve the situation of the business, its employees and customers. Without this clarity, the Salesforce team can feel overwhelmed and attention can be focused on the wrong areas, hampering the project's ability to meet the needs of the organisation.

The Salesforce delivery team member(s) need to have the professional skills of BA, Agile PM and change

---

9   Wood, J, How to be a Salesforce admin – Part 4 – How to plan a CRM roadmap (Supermums, 2022), https://supermums.org/how-to-be-a-salesforce-admin-part-4-how-to-plan-a-crm-roadmap/, accessed 4 September 2023

management to effectively facilitate the conversations needed to produce a CRM roadmap. Without this, there will be poor system adoption, integration and alignment across departments, resulting in data silos, poor customer intelligence and inconsistent information across systems. All of this undermines the value placed on the CRM and can lead to low adoption of the system.

How to plan a CRM roadmap

Understanding the strategic business priorities is the first step to determining the priorities of a CRM build; this helps to lay the foundation for creating the CRM strategy. Applying Agile project management methodologies is the most common approach used for prioritisation in technology projects. This foundation can only be put in place if there is a clear governance structure for the CRM; this is commonly called a Centre of Excellence (CoE) and is hosted by an executive sponsor.

Project governance is a crucial element of the CRM roadmap, especially for complicated and risky projects. You need a framework for making decisions about the project, defining roles, responsibilities and liabilities for the accomplishment of the project, and that governs the effectiveness of the delivery.

One of the key areas to establish is the specific role types within the framework – this will assist in ensuring clear ownership. There is often a lack of clarity around groups such as super users and admins, business analysts and the technical team. Given that these different groups should have an understanding of the technical process/design and also business processes, they will be able to assist with the validation of requirements and ensure they deliver upon the specified business metrics, as well as make key approval decisions. This will ultimately enable the development of Salesforce to be aligned to business strategy and the overall CRM roadmap.

How to prepare the client for business analysis

Depending on whether you are working internally or externally as a Salesforce professional, there are some questions you may want to ask in advance of starting any project in order to better estimate the time, budget and effort that will be required. Properly preparing the client for BA is a game changer, as it increases the amount of time they invest in planning and designing so that you can be confident you're building the right solution.

As part of this preparation, you should meet with the key sponsors and executive team to understand and prioritise the main business drivers for this implementation and to decide on the approach you are collectively going to take to elicit requirements from stakeholders. Understanding the business priorities will help to prioritise functional and technical requirements. A change management and communication plan are also essential, and your approach to BA will be governed by the organisational culture and preferred communication style of the executive team.

The main things you need to do to prepare the client for BA are:

- Advise and work with the executive sponsor on how and when to implement a suitable communication strategy to inform the stakeholders about the why, what and how of the Salesforce project, to generate buy-in.

- Explain the BA and Agile PM process in advance of a discovery workshop to anyone who is participating. Showcase a demo of the product features, explain the questions you are going to ask and how requirements can be prioritised. Record this session so that people can rewatch it as needed.

- Agree a suitable timeline by which the participants will prepare all of the information you will need before the discovery workshop, to maximise its value. There is no point running a workshop if participants turn up unprepared without the answers to your questions. This is often one of the biggest causes of project delays and budget impacts.

- Circulate a BA questionnaire in advance of the discovery workshop with a deadline for participants to complete it by, so you can review their responses before conducting the workshop and to make sure the relevant information has been prepared. You can access a whole set of Business Analysis Questionnaires on our Consultancy Skills Course.

- During the discovery workshop, present different technical scenarios and a demo to help improve processes so that participants can make informed decisions.

To make this easy for you, I have developed a four-step approach to business analysis. Follow this and you'll be a BA pro. There are also various templates (BA questionnaires and documentation) available within the Supermums Consultancy Skills course.

1. Understand the why – what is the strategy underpinning the business case for the CRM implementation?
    - Understand the business strategy
    - Complete a SWOT analysis
    - Identify the KPIs
    - Mobilise the roles and responsibilities of the executive sponsor

BUSINESS ANALYSIS

- Establish a Centre of Excellence
- Identify the business stakeholders who need to be consulted

2. Understand how the client works and what they need, then execute your BA elicitation strategy with different stakeholders. This could include:

   - Delivering demos
   - Interviews
   - Shadowing
   - Workshops
   - Questionnaires
   - Meetings
   - Focus groups
   - Document analysis

3. Record the business needs in a professional way to provide clear documentation. A suite of BA documentation would include:

   - Business canvas, explaining the business strategy
   - Business case, demonstrating the ROI for the CRM
   - CRM strategy, outlining the reasons and strategy for the CRM

- Process maps, documenting the before and after business processes
- Technical audit, documenting the different technology used by a business and how it interacts
- Stakeholder context diagram, showcasing the different stakeholders and their interaction with the various systems
- Requirements log, detailing the functional, non-functional and technical requirements with the level of prioritisation and business case
- Technical workbook, detailing all of the elements that need to be built by a technical team
- Object entity diagram, showcasing the high-level architecture of the CRM system

4. Schedule when to do BA and the CRM implementation with an agreed project management plan. Here are some questions to find answers to:

    - What are the functional requirements?
    - What are the non-functional requirements?
    - What is the MoSCoW prioritisation of requirements in line with DSDM Agile PM?

- What is the time frame to completing the requirements?
- What are the dependencies between the requirements?
- What is the budget for the overall implementation?
- What is the resource for the overall implementation?

REFLECTIVE EXERCISE

Grab a notebook and write down some thoughts on the questions below. This will help you identify what steps you need to take to boost your confidence and knowledge in BA and requirements engineering.

- How equipped and confident are you with BA skills?
- Do you have presentation templates with ready-prepared questions to facilitate design workshops?
- Do you know how to document the business case?
- Do you have a ready-made set of BA questions to ask per type of solution?
- Do you feel confident that you know how to document all the processes, requirements and technical solutions?
- Do you have systems and tools available to document, share and manage the delivery of requirements?

At the end of this chapter, you should have a better understanding of why business analysis is important and what the different approaches to gathering requirements can be.

Thank you to Slalom for sponsoring this chapter. As one of the leading global Salesforce consultancies, they are an authoritative voice in the Salesforce ecosystem.

Slalom got their start doing things differently. Instead of a gruelling, up-or-out career, they offered balance and sanity. The opportunity to love both your work and your life. To prioritise family and work on high-impact projects with companies in your community.

The founding idea was to 'Invest in people. Invest in communities. Invest in our clients' success.' Today, Slalom is a $2.4bn company with over 9,500 employees and is frequently named a 'best place to work'. Their clients include more than half the Fortune 100 and a third of the Fortune 500, along with startups, not-for-profits and innovative organisations of all kinds.

C
Change Management

> Your customer says, 'But I don't want to stop using my spreadsheets and pads.'
>
> *As a consultant, do you know how to engage and enthuse your stakeholders to buy into Salesforce?*

In this chapter, you will find out about change management principles and how to communicate with impact throughout the project life cycle.

Have you ever been in a situation where you feel uncertain about changes that are coming for reasons that you don't understand? There hasn't been a discussion, people haven't asked your opinion and you don't know what the future holds for you. You want to stick with your normal way of working – you don't know why things are changing and you don't know if the proposed changes are going to be for the better or worse. It makes you feel unsettled and unmotivated.

This is the situation that arises when you don't implement a change management strategy, to communicate the why, what, how and when of the project with all its stakeholders. If people feel unsure about what's happening, it can lead to huge adoption issues as they aren't bought into the project at any stage. In reality, you will get different types of stakeholders, some of whom will resist the changes whatever you do. There will always be winners and losers, but the key is that a change management communication strategy is an important way to mobilise the most positive response possible.

WHAT CAN GO WRONG?

Below are three challenges that can arise on projects where there has been no/poor change management. Left unresolved, these can mean the system doesn't get adopted.

1. **Top-down decision-making.** The culture of an organisation can hugely influence the approach you take to BA. One of the challenges of a machine-led culture within an organisation is that there can be top-down decision-making in which only the managers participate in the design workshops and decide the process, and end users aren't consulted in any way. This can lead to difficult training workshops as the end users are being told how to work and they don't believe the system is fit for purpose. This is always an awkward situation. A blended elicitation approach that aligns with culture is recommended to produce a better outcome.

2. **Resistance.** You need to manage resisters who don't want to listen or get engaged quickly to stop them becoming a poison ivy for the rest of the team. Escalate the situation to their manager or the executive sponsor and consider the best way to clarify the issue, and see if a resolution can be reached through coaching and discussion. In some cases, I've seen people managed out of an organisation.

3. **No ownership.** It's important to know who is owning the changes to the business process and business rules as you go through the design process. A lot of things can be discussed in the design workshops and decisions made about new ways of working, but if a client-side manager isn't leading, documenting or owning these changes themselves, then in my experience they won't remember or implement them.

HOW TO GET IT RIGHT

The management team needs to be on board with change management principles and understand their own role in getting their team members on board.

In this chapter, you will learn more about how to plan for change management in a professional way that enables you to enthuse, engage and empower stakeholders at all levels.

What is change management?

The four key principles of change management are:

1. **Understanding the organisational need, culture and readiness** – this will tell you what approach is most appropriate for the organisational culture and history.

2. **Understanding different stakeholder personalities** – this involves knowing who the different stakeholders are, as well as their different personalities and learning styles, identifying the enthusiasts and the blockers.

3. **Empowering people to lead change** – this means equipping the executive leader to lead change and creating short to long-term teams, for example a change management team, Salesforce champions and a Centre of Excellence.

4. **Implementing a project communications strategy** – this is about planning communications throughout the project, explaining the why, what and when in at least three different ways to enthuse, engage and embed.

Why is change management important for adoption? If change management principles are ignored, there is a probable chance that stakeholders won't be engaged, enthused or empowered enough to engage with the Salesforce system, because:

- The business case is not clear or communicated
- People are not clear on why the change is important and buy-in is low
- People do not feel consulted and are frustrated or disengaged

This will lead to:

- Input into the design being limited
- A poor technical solution
- The project being delayed
- User adoption being low/nil

My approach to change management

If you use my tried and tested approach to change management, you will boost adoption. At Supermums I teach four pillars of change management to maximise the success of your Salesforce project. These pillars are not linear but layered throughout the project life cycle; they are:

- Analyse
- Plan
- Strategise
- Change

Let's talk through each of these in detail.

Analyse: Understand the rationale and readiness for the Salesforce project

This pillar leads us back to the importance of BA skills, as analysis is a core component of change management. Stakeholders need to understand why the CRM project is important. They need to know the business case and rationale for undertaking the project. It's also important to understand what the right time is to do the project. A risk analysis needs to be undertaken to identify and understand the risks so that you can design and implement an effective risk mitigation strategy.

Plan: Decide on an approach and gather a change management team for the Salesforce project

This pillar relies on your Agile PM skills, as you are coordinating a change management project plan to be delivered by a change management team. The CRM PM plan needs to dovetail with the change management project plan to ensure everything is aligned. The two are fundamentally different but need to be interwoven. The focus of a change management plan is on communication to engage stakeholders. This plan will be executed by a range of people, from senior managers to HR, internal marketing, operations and governance, all of whom will make up the change management team.

Strategise: Mobilise leadership to execute the plan and engage stakeholders for the Salesforce project

Once the change management plan has been agreed, the executive sponsor and leadership team need to be mobilised by being given clear roles and responsibilities. The leaders will need to communicate to the business and teams what is happening, when and why. Management needs to be aware and bought into the strategy in advance to support the execution of the plan and communication campaigns. To enthuse, engage and empower stakeholders will require a mix of communication methods to respond to different motivational and learning styles.

Change: Prepare for the Salesforce roll-out and embed changes as the norm

In anticipation of the roll-out it's important to prepare an adoption strategy with a set of processes in place to create a carrot and stick approach for adoption. Ideally, you want users to feel enthused, empowered and engaged in the process, but you will also need to look at ways to embed these changes as the norm through institutional and compliance changes. Once a system is rolled out, how do you embed a change management culture going forward and establish quality control to check that adoption is at the expected levels, and to evaluate success?

All of these pillars are unpacked further in later chapters, and I can't wait to get into them with you. This is my favourite topic.

REFLECTIVE EXERCISE

Grab a notebook and write down some thoughts on the questions below. This will show you what steps you need to take to boost your confidence in and knowledge of change management.

- How equipped and confident are you with change management skills?
- Do you know how to assess risk, stakeholders and organisational culture?
- Do you know how to deliver and manage communications with different types of stakeholders?
- Do you have systems and tools available to facilitate change?

At the end of this chapter, you should have a better understanding of why change management is an essential ingredient in a transformation project, and how you can plan a strategic communication campaign to engage stakeholders throughout the project life cycle.

Thank you to DESelect for sponsoring this chapter. DESelect, a cloud-based SaaS provider and official Salesforce partner, has invested in creating tools to aid powerful communication strategies using their Marketing Cloud, which is the leading marketing enablement platform on the Salesforce AppExchange. Fortune 500 leaders and mid-sized businesses leverage DESelect's intuitive drag-and-drop solutions to help marketing teams combine data sources, segment audiences and power highly personalised campaigns without code or technical assistance.

D
DevOps

Your team just announced, 'Oh no, we just broke the live system.'

As a consultant, do you know how to manage the DevOps process and team?

In this chapter, we'll find out how to put a DevOps process in place.

WHAT CAN GO WRONG?

Have you ever had a deployment that fails a few times, then breaks something in your org once you finally get your changes live? The deployment might even have deleted important metadata or data in the target org. Not only is it frustrating and stressful to have to fix these problems when they arise, but they can impact the trust your clients and/or end users have in you.

HOW TO GET IT RIGHT

> No one wants to announce that they broke the live system and then be scrambling to get it fixed ASAP. A robust DevOps process helps you validate and thoroughly test a new Salesforce solution before it goes live, so you can avoid any such mishaps. DevOps can also help you undo a change quickly if something does go awry. This provides peace of mind for all deployments, but especially when deploying to live orgs.

What is Salesforce DevOps?

DevOps, a combination of development (Dev) and operations (Ops), is the industry gold standard for how companies manage their Salesforce processes. It's an Agile way of working that empowers all Salesforce professionals to contribute to the development and release cycle, whatever their technical skills or role.

Among its core objectives, DevOps aims to:

- Improve collaboration between admins, developers and business stakeholders
- Speed up deployments and testing along an automated release pipeline
- Enhance the quality and reliability of new features and functionality

- Increase the frequency of releases to production
- Build resilience with full visibility into changes, including options for rollback and disaster recovery

DevOps brings significant benefits to businesses, helping them to get the most out of their Salesforce investment. More frequent releases, for example, mean teams can respond quickly and in a flexible way to changing business needs and opportunities. By continuously delivering small improvements and iteratively building out new functionality, teams are better able to respond to business priorities while incorporating continual feedback from stakeholders.

At the heart of this process, Git-based version control gives teams a powerful way to collaborate on and coordinate a complex pipeline with multiple contributors and different streams of development and customisation. Using a DevOps platform like Gearset, each contributor can interact with version control using clicks not code, pushing changes to release and keeping all teams' development environments in sync.

Version control also makes it possible to add automation to workflows, which dramatically reduces the huge amounts of time teams otherwise have to spend on manual and error-prone processes, such as deployments and testing. In turn, this frees up teams to spend more time adding value for their end users.

The impact of successful DevOps

As well as producing a whole host of business benefits, DevOps is also critical for avoiding costly mistakes. When the principles of DevOps are applied, Salesforce teams not only minimise the risk to their orgs but also strengthen their ability to recover from faulty deployments. Here are two real-life examples:

- **Introducing a breaking change.** New changes can impact Salesforce functionality like online payment processes, meaning people can't donate or buy at a given point. This obviously has a hugely detrimental impact on sales income and the organisation as a whole. Robust testing through a DevOps workflow reduces the chance that you'll deploy a bug to production, and version control means you can quickly revert a deployment if an issue does arise. Minimal downtime makes for a happy business and end users.

- **Lost data that can't be recovered.** Data loss is a nightmare scenario — but it's a reality that many teams face. You don't want to be in a situation where your deployment or data import is responsible for losing business-critical data. A mature DevOps process includes an incident detection strategy and a pre-planned recovery process, to ensure you have an easy way to restore lost data and metadata.

Who is DevOps for?

DevOps expertise isn't just for the specialists. Precisely because DevOps is all about collaboration, the demand for talent is there at all levels. Whether you're seeking a new role as an admin, developer, architect or consultant, understanding core DevOps concepts, tools and workflows can get you a long way and help you to progress your career.

Opportunities for professionals with DevOps knowledge currently exist across all industries and types of company. Larger organisations and enterprises with bigger Salesforce teams and more complex processes are especially likely to need DevOps know-how and will pay a premium for that expertise.

DevOps has become the industry standard. As the Salesforce ecosystem realises the limitations and challenges of traditional org-to-org development methods, familiarity with DevOps tools is rapidly becoming essential. In fact, DevOps is now a job role in its own right, with companies hiring Salesforce DevOps specialists at an attractive salary band.

Given that DevOps can accelerate Salesforce development while also decreasing bugs and issues, it's no surprise that organisations are so willing to invest in DevOps tools and practices, to help retain their competitive edge.

How to get DevOps right

Learning about Salesforce DevOps is a gradual process and, as with any discipline, specialist expertise requires practical experience. As a broad outline, the following are the tools, concepts and processes you will become familiar with as you make progress on your DevOps journey.

As a **beginner**, you will:

- Learn about development on Salesforce and modern release management
- Practise deploying different metadata types between orgs
- Back up your data and metadata

As a **novice**, you will:

- Get to grips with the fundamentals of version control
- Start using a Git hosting provider, eg GitHub
- Practice committing metadata to version control

As a **practitioner**, you will:

- Build up a repository of Salesforce metadata
- Begin treating version control as the 'source of truth' for development

- Explore the benefits of different Git-branching strategies

As an **expert**, you will:

- Automate tests, monitoring and deployment steps in the release process
- Seed sandboxes with masked production data for more robust testing
- Learn about the tools available from Salesforce DX

As a **luminary**, you will:

- Ensure compliance with backups integrated into the release process
- Create a fast-flowing CI/CD pipeline you can visualise in one place

Advance your career with Salesforce DevOps

The rapid adoption of Salesforce DevOps by companies across all industries and sizes is opening up exciting career opportunities for both new entrants and seasoned professionals in the Salesforce jobs market. Getting ahead of the game could be a smart career move, as adding DevOps knowledge and expertise to your Salesforce skill set will set you apart from the crowd and could put you on a lucrative path.

A great place to learn all about Salesforce DevOps is on the free training platform DevOps Launchpad. Here, you'll find industry-relevant courses and certifications for the Salesforce community, written by DevOps experts. Whether you're new to Salesforce, or have years of experience, there are resources that cover all aspects of DevOps, including certification tracks in Salesforce DevOps fundamentals and Salesforce DevOps leadership. The courses are broken down into bite-sized learning items with short quizzes to test your knowledge, enabling you to learn at your own pace and in your own time. You can download your certificates to add to your résumé and social profiles to demonstrate your skills.

DevOps Launchpad has been developed by Gearset, but the vast majority of the content is vendor-agnostic, designed to give you a solid understanding of core DevOps concepts and best practices. If you're a beginner, it will help you get up and running with DevOps, or if you've some experience it can help you improve your existing processes. Find a link in the book resources page on our website.

DEVOPS

At the end of this chapter, you should have a better understanding of the important part DevOps plays in the project life cycle to ensure that changes to the system are communicated and managed intentionally before go-live.

Thank you to Gearset for sponsoring this chapter. Gearset are the leading experts in DevOps and DevOps education with their DevOps Launchpad platform, which provides powerful solutions for metadata and CPQ deployments, CI/CD, automated testing, sandbox seeding and backups. It helps Salesforce teams apply DevOps best practices to their development and release process, so they can rapidly and securely deliver higher-quality projects. DevOps Launchpad is a free training platform for all areas of Salesforce DevOps, to upskill the Salesforce community through practical training and certification.

PART THREE
FORMING A TEAM

E
Evaluating The Opportunity

> You are asking the customer, 'Is this organisation really bought into using Salesforce?'
>
> *As the consultant, do you know how to assess whether the organisation is culturally onboard and committed to investing in their Salesforce project?*

In this chapter, you'll find out what questions you need to ask when you go for an interview or pitch for a new project.

When you are considering taking up an opportunity to lead a Salesforce project, I want you to turn the tables on the interview process. Typically, you would focus on selling yourself to an organisation, which quite rightly you will have to do, but I also want you evaluate whether it is actually a project you want to lead.

Does it have the right ingredients in place to make the recipe a success?

You should ask questions about the business, people and environment, as well as the team's appetite for Salesforce. In essence, you are doing the first stage of BA using the POPIT and risk analysis frameworks before even committing to doing the project.

Know that it is OK to walk away from a project if there are warning signs that the ingredients aren't right. While it can feel great if they select you, trust your judgement if you feel it's not for you.

WHAT CAN GO WRONG?

> Be concerned if you walk into an interview where the people interviewing you don't smile or try to build any rapport with you. Where it's all very serious and corporate and the focus is on them selecting you. Ultimately, you will be working extremely closely with these people and acting as their trusted adviser. Within this type of job role, you need to feel there is a good energy and level of respect and how they show up at interview is indicative of how they will be throughout the project.

HOW TO GET IT RIGHT

It's good to get clarity on the resourcing plan and budget allocated to an internal Salesforce admin team for management of the system beyond implementation. If there isn't enough resource to manage the CRM internally then there will be problems long term, as there is no one to own or manage the system. There also has be a commitment to governance of the CRM and an understanding of the four roles of a Salesforce admin that I cover in later chapters.

Make sure there is a great executive sponsor onboard who can communicate the business case, the allocated budget and explain any risks involved. If there is no clear executive sponsor with the right authority or commitment to the role, this can result in a digital belly flop as the rest of the employees and managers won't get on board.

In this chapter, I will provide twenty-six questions to ask when you go for an interview or pitch to lead a new Salesforce project.

Questions to ask at interview

To kick the conversation off you can ask some intelligent questions based on the Supermums Risk Register, which we teach in our Consultancy Skills Course. It uses the NLP Logical Level Methodology that explores where issues or pain points may arise in a situation, a model that can be easily applied to a Salesforce project.

```
        Purpose
        Identity
    Values and Belief
       Capabilities
        Behaviour
       Environment
```

NLP Logical Level Methodology

Asking these questions will help you assess if the job represents a risk for you, but equally shows your intelligence around risk mitigation. Your interviewers will certainly be impressed.

Start with the following:

1. **Purpose** – how do you see Salesforce transforming your organisation? What is its purpose? The ideal answer is that they see Salesforce as fundamentally changing the way their company does business and serves customers – it's going to be transformational.

2. **Identity** – how is the management team going to use Salesforce to manage performance? How are

EVALUATING THE OPPORTUNITY

staff responding to the introduction or adoption of Salesforce? The ideal answer is that they see Salesforce as the beating heart of the organisation and relish the idea of real-time performance analysis and everyday business use.

3. **Beliefs/values** – what benefits do the different teams/departments expect that Salesforce offers/will offer them? The ideal answer will demonstrate that there is a clear business case for designated departments and that team members are bought into the solution and not opposing its use.

4. **Capabilities** – who does the Salesforce technical team comprise of? If they already use Salesforce, how confident are they in using it currently? If they don't use it already, do team members know what Salesforce is? The ideal answer is that they have more than one technical team member in-house and have Salesforce champions per department. From user confidence level you can gauge whether further training is needed.

5. **Behaviour** – what is the preferred approach to BA to inform the development of Salesforce? If they use Salesforce already, are their clear processes mapped out? The ideal answer will demonstrate that they have or want to invest time in BA and that they want to add value to their existing processes. If you are walking into an existing implementation you would ideally want to see a roadmap of the work undertaken.

6. **Environment** – how are the team using Salesforce currently? Is it via an office, or virtually? Do they work via mobiles/tablets/laptops? Is Salesforce to be integrated with other technical systems? Their answer will show you whether they have a clear idea of the technical landscape and you will get an overview of what other systems need to interact with Salesforce or be replaced. This might indicate how technically advanced the project is.

We also went out to the wider Salesforce community and asked them for their question suggestions, which you can find below, split into categories.

Contextual questions:

7. What does the roadmap for Salesforce look like right now?

8. What are the top projects/priorities you're looking for the person in this role to tackle in the next year?

9. What are the company's concerns about Salesforce right now?

10. What challenges will I face in this role?

11. Could I install a free organisation analysis tool that looks at the meta data to see the current status of product and user adoption?

12. Can you show me some examples of your process/config documentation?
13. Who has stayed at the company the longest? You can then direct a follow up question at that individual, something like: 'Salesforce career paths are in high demand; what about this company or its leaders has kept you here so long?'

Managing Salesforce:

14. What's the decision-making process and who is the decision maker when it comes to Salesforce changes? This question alone can reveal a lot about the position and highlight potential red flags.
15. How often do you deploy changes? What does the schedule look like?
16. What tools/infrastructure do you use to manage Salesforce changes? This relates to everything from backup to developer Integrated Development Environments (IDEs).
17. What's the user to admin ratio? With this question, you're checking there aren't too many users to look after by yourself.
18. How deep is your backlog? This will let you find out what work there is to do, whether too much or too little.

19. What are the primary skills and products you are looking at, so that I can do some more prep on those areas?

Finally, you can ask questions about your role:

20. What will my typical day look like?

21. Will you cover the cost of my certificates/training? Will I get time allocated to study?

22. What are your KPIs for this role and progression/reward structure?

23. Who do I report to? Who does my direct manager report to? Does my direct manager have decision-making power, or is he/she only there to give me tasks?

24. What's the performance/appraisal cycle? (Some companies have an annual and some a biannual cycle.)

25. What is the work–life balance here? Do you have options to work remotely/from home?

26. If there a bonus or commission scheme?

After completing this chapter, you should feel confident in evaluating a Salesforce project to decide if it's the right one for you. Remember, the client needs to sell the opportunity to you as much as you need to sell yourself to them. It's a two-way street to achieving Salesforce success.

F
Four Roles Of An Awesome Admin

> Your customer asks, 'What do I need to do as the Salesforce admin?'
>
> *As a consultant, do you know how to empower a Salesforce admin with an action plan to manage the system?*

In this chapter, find out more about the four roles and forty tasks of an awesome admin.

You've decided you want to pursue the opportunity and you've taken up the mantle to lead the Salesforce project. Congratulations! At this stage, you want to make sure you have one or more Salesforce administrators in post regardless of whether it's a new or existing implementation. The Salesforce administrator function could be being delivered by you or someone else, but as the Salesforce consultant you should make it your responsibility to ensure there is a good core team in place to manage the system long term. This could mean upskilling people as Salesforce administrators, or it could mean hiring new people to cover this role. Either way, making sure they have the right training and skills is critical for success.

Salesforce recommend the following user to admin ratios:

Number of users	Administration resources
1–30 users	< 1 full-time administrator
31–74 users	1+ full-time administrator
75–149 users	1 senior administrator; one junior administrator
140–499 users	1 business analyst, 2–4 administrators

WHAT CAN GO WRONG?

> If someone has been appointed as the Salesforce admin but they have no skills, they won't know what to do in their job role or how to do it. This will mean the system and users are not supported until this level of skill is in place.

> There can be a problem if there is insufficient Salesforce admin staff to cover proactive and reactive admin work, meaning that the Salesforce admin will get overwhelmed and burnt out and users will get frustrated. There needs to be a high degree of rigour around prioritisation or an increase in investment in resources.

Compliance requirements can get left unattended if the Salesforce admin focuses their time on the 'fun' stuff and urgent cases, and is ignorant of all of the other responsibilities as it's not something they enjoy or have scheduled in their diary.

HOW TO GET IT RIGHT

To ensure nothing is missed and you have the right admins doing all of the right things, download our free Salesforce Administrator Action Plan from the book resources page. This explains the four roles and forty tasks of a Salesforce admin; you can share this with your admin(s) or use it yourself.

The four roles of a Salesforce admin

What does it mean to be a Salesforce admin? An admin can wear many hats, and the variety of tasks in the role can be rewarding but sometimes overwhelming.

Being a Salesforce administrator is an important responsibility, especially if you are in sole charge of managing a system. Your role will entail managing the CRM system and its data, keeping it secure and trusted, while also developing a system that meets the needs of the team and can perform now and in the future.

To help administrators get clear on their responsibilities I have compiled a list of forty tasks that a Salesforce administrator would typically need to think about when managing a system.

I presented on how to be an awesome admin at Dreamforce in 2019 and talked about the four personas of an #awesomeadmin; these correspond to the different roles.

The four roles and personas are:

1. **Security Management.** Imagine yourself as the **Guardian** of the system, protecting who has access, when and how, to what. Within security management, considerations at a strategic level include data management, user access and password policies. Failure to manage data securely could result in a data breach, financial penalties, reputational risk and, in the worst case, personal liabilities.

2. **System Management.** Imagine yourself as the **Doctor** for the system, undertaking health

checks, triaging problems and prescribing solutions. Within system management, considerations at a strategic level include case management, error logs and critical updates. Failure to manage a system properly could result in automation fails, customer issues, reputation risk and user frustration.

3. **Data Management.** Imagine yourself as the **Housekeeper** of the system, keeping all of the data nice and tidy for the users to trust and use effectively. Within data management, considerations at a strategic level include data integrity, business rules and data deletion. Failure to manage data properly can result in poor data integrity, which in turn can lead to low user trust/adoption, poor customer intelligence and unusable performance management data.

4. **CRM RoadMap.** Imagine yourself as the **Leader** of the CRM strategy. You need to look to the future and sell a vision that benefits the success of your organisation and team. By leading a CRM roadmap, you are learning and educating your organisation on the possibilities to empower users to use and evolve their system by introducing or integrating new functionality or systems to maximise business value. Failure to share knowledge and possibilities with colleagues internally can result in multiple systems, data silos, lack of customer intelligence, poor business performance and low value in CRM.

The responsibilities of a Salesforce admin

One of the best approaches to managing the responsibilities of the admin role is to implement a regular schedule of weekly, monthly and quarterly tasks and to schedule them in your diary to ensure these tasks get done. It's all too easy for regular routine 'boring' tasks to be forgotten about in favour of new and exciting feature developments. The risk here is that while new features are being developed, the system's data could be getting dirty and users losing trust in using the system. If you take your eye off the ball, the whole system can cascade.

Below is a quick overview of the responsibilities a great Salesforce admin will be keeping up with.

Daily/Weekly Tasks	Monthly Tasks	Quarterly Tasks
User management	Cyber security	Health checks
Error handling	GDPR compliance	Release updates
Support desk	Data cleansing	Training
Duplicate management	Data validation	Centre of Excellence
DevOps	Business analysis	Business priorities
	Return on investment	CRM roadmap

At the end of this chapter, you should have a clear understanding of and strategy for the Salesforce administrator function and role, so that they/you know exactly what to do on a regular basis to proactively maintain a clean, healthy and secure system.

Thank you to GridMate for sponsoring this chapter. If you need to improve the user navigation and experience of your Salesforce system for end users, they have a range of products that can help.

GridMate is a powerful productivity suite of over thirty components that has revolutionised the way users work in Salesforce. Designed to enhance the user experience, it is built on the lightning framework with an easy-to-use interface that allows users to quickly and efficiently create, edit and manage their data. Users can streamline their workflow, reduce errors and improve data accuracy, while also saving time and increasing productivity.

With spreadsheet-like inline editing capabilities and an enhanced 360-degree view of your data providing a single source of truth in one pane, users can reduce clicks by over 93% and customise how they visualise data.

GridMate is a game changer for businesses that rely on Salesforce. With its intuitive design, powerful user experience enhancements and ability to improve productivity, it is ideal for getting the most out of your Salesforce investment and increasing utilisation within your organisation.

G
Governance

> Your customer asks, 'How do we get new Salesforce requirements signed off?'
>
> *As a consultant, do you know how to establish governance and a Centre of Excellence for managing Salesforce long term?*

In this chapter, you'll learn how to put in place a governance team and process to manage the CRM roadmap.

Managing Salesforce is a team effort and involves buy-in at all levels of the organisation to support ongoing success, whether you're a solo admin or a wider team. This is where a Salesforce CoE comes in. Never heard of it before? Let me explain.

A Salesforce CoE basically acts as a central governing body for the entire organisation. It brings together stakeholders from across the organisation to create a single, well-defined group that is responsible for making decisions when it comes to Salesforce.

WHAT CAN GO WRONG?

Without an effective CoE, you may struggle to:

- Prioritise requests and workload
- Get sign-off for new products, features and requirements
- Secure resources for developing the CRM
- Get different teams/departments bought into the CRM
- Design and roll out a CRM roadmap for the future
- Report on the ROI of the CRM
- Maximise user adoption if communication is unclear

HOW TO GET IT RIGHT

In this chapter, I will share tips on how to set up a governance structure to support the ongoing planning, management and maintenance of the Salesforce system to reduce user frustration and poor adoption.

The key functions of a CoE are summarised in the diagram below:

GOVERNANCE

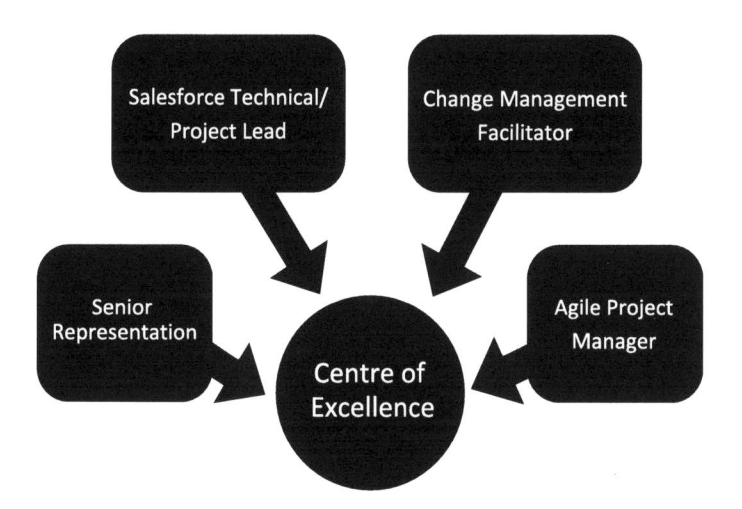

Functions of the Centre of Excellence

The CoE is responsible for the CRM strategy, managing governance and setting and evaluating the metrics of success. They determine the allocation of suitable resources and priorities for investment and the time of the technical team. Typically, the group would meet monthly or quarterly, depending on the level of transformation taking place.

Essential ingredients for the Centre of Excellence

The CoE is made up of several essential ingredients. We'll run through each of these in turn.

CRM strategy, roadmap and action plan

The CRM strategy clearly outlines the business case and performance metrics that the CRM is expected to support, with stages of implementation and justification for investment. It should facilitate decision-making to create a detailed roadmap, agreed deliverables and a clear progress report on ROI.

An executive sponsor

A CoE also needs an executive sponsor. How effective the executive sponsor is can make or break the Salesforce project. If there is a low level of executive sponsorship and they don't perform the tasks needed, it can derail the project from the start as issues are allowed to cascade throughout the whole project:

- Low executive sponsorship leads to poor communication
- Poor communication leads to low engagement
- Low engagement leads to poor design
- Poor design leads to low benefits
- Low benefits lead to low adoption

But if you turn the situation on its head, a high level of executive sponsorship gives the project the best chance of success:

- High executive sponsorship leads to great communication
- Great communication leads to high engagement
- High engagement leads to great design
- Great design leads to great benefits
- Great benefits lead to high adoption

As the Salesforce consultant, it is wise to upward manage the executive sponsor to check they understand what their role entails. Below I've provided a handy process to explain the vital roles and responsibilities of an executive sponsor that you can discuss and share with your client.

Key Roles for the Executive Sponsor	Techniques	Outcome
Define the Vision	Rationale for change and the ideal for the future.	Awareness
	Use storytelling, demos, statistics, case studies, reality check, business case, goal setting.	Understanding
	Acknowledge any loss to empathise, or preservation of existing features to reassure.	A sense of urgency

(Continued)

(Cont)

Key Roles for the Executive Sponsor	Techniques	Outcome
Mobilise Resources	Create momentum to produce change. Build a team, generate management buy-in from frontline to executive level, allocate finances, and set a clear direction.	Shows something is going to happen.
Implementation Strategy	Work with and transfer ownership to the team to gather input from all stakeholders, to identify how and when it is going to happen through goal setting, action planning, facilitation, research, negotiation, consultation, and project management.	Clarity on when, how, what and by whom, to ensure it is realised.
Communication Strategy	Identify a range of communication methods to create two-way communication channels - electronic, mobile, social, paper, verbal - 1-1, open space technology, World Cafés, Future Search, feedback loops, conflict-resolution, dialogue.	Awareness, and encourages engagement throughout the change process to generate buy-in and adoption.

Cross-departmental team

A CoE requires a cross-departmental decision-making team with bottom–up and top–down representation. This team should consist of:

- An **internal leader**, who should be appointed as the executive sponsor. They will typically lead the CoE representing the business vision, goals and priorities.

- **Senior management representatives**, who are responsible for sponsorship, BA, compliance and/or adoption of Salesforce CRM within their department or cross-departments.

- **Salesforce technical/project lead,** who will have oversight of the roadmap, project development and the backlog informed by on-the-ground BA and the technical implementation team. They are responsible for communicating new requirements, agreeing prioritisation and reporting on work in progress or completed.

- **Agile project management lead**, who will manage the what, when and how of things scheduled for implementation, with oversight of internal and external influences.

- **Change management lead**, who will manage a communication strategy to communicate the why, what and when of digital transformation changes, with input from senior exec level to the Salesforce team.

Understanding and mitigating risks

We want the client and, mostly importantly, the members of the CoE to feel prepared for implementing and managing a CRM long term and to make it a success, as, ultimately, it's their reputation at stake as well as your own.

Based on my experience, one of the most important elements of any project is educating a client about all the risks upfront and helping to mitigate them where possible. Quite often, these people may not have been involved in a CRM implementation before, so they do not know the risks. It is, therefore, hard for them to put together their own risk register and so it is much easier if we give them a template to complete with typical risks, impacts and mitigation strategies so that they can identify, understand, assess, rank and act on the risks accordingly.

To help my trainees, I've put together a comprehensive twenty-point Risk Analysis Register that I encourage them to complete with the executive sponsor and CoE team. Below is a quick summary of the twenty risks it addresses:

GOVERNANCE

1. Have they appointed an internal project manager at the client organisation?
2. Have they identified an internal Salesforce admin(s) at the start of the project?
3. Is the Salesforce admin going to be equipped with adequate training?
4. Are there enthused Salesforce champions appointed for each department/team?
5. Is there commitment and buy-in to completing Salesforce Trailheads?
6. Is there buy-in to the 'train the trainer' approach with champions?
7. Do they have resource appointed to manage data cleansing?
8. What is the level of Salesforce experience among client stakeholders?
9. What is the capacity of staff to evaluate their processes and business needs in readiness for the design process?
10. Do they have suitable Wi-Fi and IT hardware to access Salesforce CRM?
11. Is the organisation ready for change and are employees bought in?
12. Is there any evidence of concern or negative resistance to a new CRM?

13. Is there a lack of clarity or alignment with Agile PM?

14. Is there any lack of clarity on the tangible business goals and benefits of the CRM implementation?

15. Is there any lack of clarity on the roles and responsibilities of an executive sponsor?

16. Could decision-making take longer than usual due to remote planning and team working?

17. Is there a risk that project tasks could be delayed and impact timelines?

18. How complex is the technical solution and are there risks in the unknown/decisions/resources?

19. Is there adequate resource/budget to manage the CRM post-implementation?

20. Has this risk register been completed and understood by the client?

Investment in business analysis

The Salesforce technical/project lead will prepare for CoE meetings by collating high-level requirements, estimated effort and the associated business case by working closely with a delivery team. Individuals may wear one or multiple hats in this function, but the common roles are:

- Salesforce champions – these are representatives within departments who oversee user adoption, identify challenges, uncover requirements and report these to the senior managers.

- Business analysts – these elicit detailed requirements with teams/departments to produce the business case and requirement log.

- The Salesforce technical team – this team is responsible for building and managing the system day to day, to understand the progress, challenges and outcomes.

Completing this chapter, you should have the clarity to communicate what the internal governance and Salesforce management function should include in order to mitigate risks and manage the system post-implementation. This is an area I can provide further support on if there is a need for guidance and training of the COE Team.

H
Hiring A Team

> Your customer asks, 'How do I find and select Salesforce professionals?'
>
> *As a Salesforce consultant, do you know how to attract and interview Salesforce professionals?*

In this chapter, you'll learn how to support a client to hire talent into Salesforce roles.

As the Salesforce consultant working either in-house or externally, you might need to help the client hire a team to work with or around you. The client may not have hired Salesforce professionals before and might not even know what job roles they need in place, so you'll need to know how to guide them in this.

WHAT CAN GO WRONG?

The three big things that can go wrong here are:

- Hiring people without the necessary certifications or experience
- The client fails to attract anyone to the job ads as their specs and salaries are not aligned
- The client doesn't have the support they need to ask the right questions in interviews or make an informed decision about whether someone is a good fit

HOW TO GET IT RIGHT

To get hiring right, it's important that you understand what job roles are needed; these should complement your own role and skills.

Here are some of the common job roles, which quite often end up having a range of different job titles:

- A business analyst focuses on asking questions, listening to people's needs and gathering requirements.
- The Salesforce architect will focus on designing the solution to meet these needs.
- The Salesforce admin gets busy building the system with clicks.
- A Salesforce developer advances the build with more technical skills.

- The project manager liaises with the different parties, making sure all of the team members work together to keep things running on time and within budget.
- The Salesforce consultant can be a hybrid of these roles – playing all or one of these roles.
- A change management consultant will be responsible for managing the communication plan of the why, what, when and how of the project.

To help with hiring, you can download a sample of job specs and interview guides from our book resources page:

In the rest of this chapter, our general manager at Supermums, Melonie Debenham, shares her top tips for hiring well.

How to interview

Before you go to market to see what candidates are available, consider how you will assess the skills of any candidates. If you have someone already in post with Salesforce knowledge, do not hesitate to ask them to help, as they will be able to provide detailed information. If you are still going through the implementation with a Salesforce consultancy, they should also be able to offer some structure to the interview process. If you are working with a recruiter to find you the right talent, then they too should be able to offer an insight into how to get the best from the interview process.

It's usual for the interview process to have more than one stage. The first interview is typically a 'get to know you' opportunity and a chance to discuss the candidate's background, ambitions and experience. The second is often a more technically based interview, usually a technical assessment or a review of a case study. The technical interview gives you as the hirer the opportunity to ensure that the candidate has the practical skills to find a solution to a problem, and the communication skills to effectively give feedback.

If you work with a recruiter, such as Supermums Consulting, they can help before and during the interview process. For example, they can screen candidates before presenting them to the client, and check certifications and qualifications. A Salesforce-specific recruiter will understand each Salesforce role and can effectively question candidates to gain the best overview of their level of understanding. It's not just about the technical skills, though; it is also important to understand the motivations as to why a candidate is applying; what their short- and long-term ambitions are. You need to know the type of organisation culture a candidate is looking to join, so that you can match the job role, skills set and cultural fit. That way, you are more likely to get a candidate that will stay with you for the long term.

How to sell your organisation

In the current market, it's important to consider that an interview is a two-way process – it is your chance, as the hirer, to establish more about the candidate, but also for the candidate to establish more about the role and the organisation they will be working within. Salesforce talent is hard to come by, and it is not unusual for a candidate to have three or four other job opportunities and interviews pending at any one time. It is, therefore, important to know how you will promote your/the client's organisation to make it stand out from the crowd.

Below are a few unique selling points that would stand out to a candidate:

- A greenfield site implementation – this means it is implementing a brand-new Salesforce system.
- Award-winning organisation – has the organisation won any awards for employee management, innovation, customer service etc?
- Global enterprise leader – is it a FTSE corporate brand with ambitious Salesforce projects?

- High-growth company – does the company have ambitious growth plans to scale globally?

- Specialist niche – is the company a specialist in a niche product or industry that could attract someone keen to specialise?

- Mission-led – is it a non-profit or mission-led company that gives back to causes?

- Benefits – does the company offer great benefits, pay or flexibility?

- CRM roadmap – is there an existing roadmap for the company in terms of implementing different Salesforce products or third-party apps that will broaden someone's portfolio and résumé?

Aiming for diversity in talent acquisition

It is best practice to strive for a gender-balanced team across your company, not just in the tech team, though the number of women available and represented in tech is a lot lower than in other areas. It is thus important to go the extra mile in making sure you have the right policies and benefits in place to attract, retain and progress women in your Salesforce team.

To help with this, I have created a forty-step action plan for attracting, retaining and progressing women in the tech sector. This can be used with and for organisations and employers to help enable better representation of women in this sector.

[QR code: SCAN ME]

Going to market to find Salesforce talent can be tough, as talent is bombarded with opportunities and so can be snapped up quickly. At the end of this chapter, you should have adequate information to be able to attract, identify and hire the best talent, plus some resources for support if you need it.

1
Identify And Upskill Salesforce Champions

> Your customer asks, 'What are Salesforce champions and who should they be?'
>
> *As a consultant, do you know how to select and manage Salesforce champions to support user adoption?*

In this chapter, you'll learn how to formalise the role of your Salesforce champions within a clear structure.

A Salesforce champion is going to be a representative of Salesforce within their team or department while also doing their existing job role. This creates a wider Salesforce support team under a central Salesforce admin function, as these champions become the go to people for issues, ideas and solutions, with different levels of responsibility.

You are identifying existing staff to be your champions as opposed to hiring new staff, and you need to follow a process, not just select people on the cuff. For Salesforce champions to achieve success, you want to make sure you select the people with the right skills, personalities, experience and motivation. At the end of the day, they are going to be the internal Salesforce power team.

WHAT CAN GO WRONG?

> If there aren't any champions, the company can suffer from low user adoption without knowing about it, as teams can get frustrated with issues arising but don't know how to flag it or to whom.
>
> If there aren't any delegated admin champions, the central Salesforce admin team can be too busy to deal with all of the issues and training, as resource is too stretched.
>
> If there is a lack of any formal structure, without clear roles and responsibilities, champions might not do anything as they don't know what is expected of them.

HOW TO GET IT RIGHT

> Salesforce champions are such a valuable resource when you get it right. It's impossible for a central in-house Salesforce admin team to have eyes and ears in all of the departments using Salesforce, so champions help to spread the love and increase adoption company-wide.

Champions can also provide cover when the central Salesforce admins are off on holiday or sick. On a day-to-day basis, champions should support end users to utilise the system properly everyday – they are someone in the user's department who understands how they work and how they should use Salesforce in their specific job.

Roles and responsibilities of a champion

A champion can have different levels of responsibility, from facilitating meetings to becoming a delegated admin. The role can offer progression where they start doing a few things, and then get more responsibilities as they train up in Salesforce administration and gain business analyst skills.

Typical champion responsibilities include:

- Facilitating team discussions to identify current challenges or improvements desired by Salesforce users, with a view to trying to resolve them.

- Providing onboarding training to new team members on how to use Salesforce.

- Analysing user adoption and troubleshooting issues.

- Managing duplicates and data integrity.

- Undertaking BA workshops and mapping out processes with the team.
- Working with managers to produce a business case for new requirements.
- Making changes to the Salesforce system to meet users' needs.
- Updating training resources if the system is updated.

How to select Salesforce champions

I would highly recommend you conduct an interview process for champions. It can be easy to simply pick the most enthusiastic person in the room, but they might not have the right skills. It can also be difficult to just nominate someone, as they might not be interested. The champion doesn't have to be senior in terms of their experience, but they have to want to do the role.

How are you going to motivate someone to apply for the role who has the relevant enthusiasm and skills? Can you offer additional benefits – an increase in salary, promotional opportunity, training?

You ideally want to advertise the opportunity amongst the team and then go through a shortlisting and interview process. Here, you will be looking for:

- **Skills:** if they have some Salesforce admin experience already then that's great, but otherwise you would be looking for someone that is good at learning technology quickly and enjoys improving business processes to produce better outcomes for the team and customer.

- **Personality:** typically you are looking for a good listener, questioner and problem-solver.

- **Experience:** ideally, they would have had experience with Salesforce and CRMs before, but this isn't essential, just a 'nice to have'. You're also looking for experience of training individuals.

- **Motivation:** individuals are motivated by reward, so the opportunity to upskill, earn more and be promoted will appeal.

How to upskill champions

How you upskill your champions depends on the roles and responsibilities you want the champion to have. If you want them to understand Salesforce but not be an actual administrator, you could get them to complete the Salesforce Associate Certification with relevant Trailheads to do.

If you want them to be a delegated Salesforce administrator, then you should encourage them to complete the Salesforce Admin Certification. If you want them to produce business cases and conduct BA, the Business Analysis Certification would be a good option. The training they undertake should suit their learning style; for example, some will prefer live training, others who like reading things may want to do Trails instead.

You can find out more about the training courses we offer on the resources page for this book:

How to manage champions

Champions are part of the governance structure. As a representative for their team and department they need to collate issues and business priorities and report this back to the Salesforce team and CoE. They shouldn't participate directly in CoE meetings, but they should have regular meetings with the in-house Salesforce team to discuss progress.

It's important to give your champions the opportunity to learn and discuss Salesforce learning, products, problems and issues with their peers and to feel like a team rather than work in isolation. To this end, it can

IDENTIFY AND UPSKILL SALESFORCE CHAMPIONS

be useful to arrange informal Salesforce lunches to get your champions together to discuss certifications, new features and tools. You could also invite them to user group meet-ups.

There will need to be an element of performance management in regard to this role as it's not an informal one; there are job responsibilities and so there needs to be a feedback loop with their direct line manager. Champions should have performance objectives, KPIs and learning opportunities built into the role.

An internal Salesforce support desk can coordinate all the different cases amongst champions, especially if they have a delegated admin role. They can respond to and update cases that are relevant for their team and department.

A communication and file-sharing platform is valuable to keep conversations going and lines of communication open so that people can discuss any of the above factors between official meetings. When you all work in different departments it can be easy to get siloed. Having a platform for communication and sharing files related to Salesforce work is imperative to good teamwork.

At the end of this chapter, you have all the information you need to be able to identify suitable champions and put a framework in place to support them in their role as a bridge between the Salesforce team and departmental users.

J
Job Roles And Responsibilities

> Your customer states, 'Things are feeling a little crazy and unclear for us.'
>
> *As a consultant, do you know how to set up a project team for success?*

This chapter will explain how to establish a high-performing team.

Building a high-performing Salesforce project team requires thought and skill. You are going to have a mix of stakeholders from the client side and potentially your own consultancy team too.

There may be both familiar and unfamiliar faces in the room and new relationships might need to be built, but they all have one thing in common. It's a new project with new objectives, roles, and responsibilities.

A Salesforce consultant needs to know how to build a team that can deliver results. With this in mind, I encourage you to look beyond what it says about the roles and responsibilities of a job on paper and instead think about what an effective team looks like.

WHAT CAN GO WRONG?

> If you don't get the team composition right for a project, things can stall or, worse, fail. It will be stressful, frustrating and awkward. It's not going to be the happy job you wanted.

HOW TO GET IT RIGHT

> Building a team for a Salesforce project is similar to building a team for any department, as you're looking for much the same traits, but the difference is you have to get the team up and running quickly and execute on your deliverables to a time and budget in order to impress your clients. There are extra pressures and expectations put upon you right away.
>
> In this chapter, I'll teach you how to set up a high-performing team structure. This includes how to recruit the right team composition, how to lay down the foundations for the team and how to ride the rollercoaster of team dynamics.

How to recruit the right roles

Below is a summary of the different roles you might want on your team. As a Salesforce consultant, you might wear a few of these hats yourself.

Business	Experts	Enablers
Ambassador	Technical experts	Trainers
Champion	Change management consultants	Coaches
Analyst	Project management	Facilitators
	Communications	Counsellors
	Specialists	

Getting the right mix of skills and attributes is important when building a team. I recommend using tools such as DISC, BELBIN, Talent Dynamics or the Myers-Briggs test to get the right mix of personalities within the job roles. Too many people with the same type of personality can skew performance. It's important for team members to respect and appreciate what each person brings to the table.

Team dynamics and relationships

Robin and Christine Glaser identified five elements that contribute to a team's level of effectiveness or ineffectiveness over time.[10] When establishing the

---

10   R Glaser and C Glaser, *Team Effectiveness Profile* (King of Prussia, 1992)

team structure, considering these elements will help you to build a high-functioning team.

Element	Outcome
Team mission	Sense of purpose
	Clarity on goals
	Clear direction
Team roles	Clear roles and responsibilities
	Understanding of others' roles
	Individual accountability for tasks
Team operating processes	Team collaboration and participation
	Appropriate frequency, timing and agenda of meetings
	An effective problem-solving and decision-making process
	Ground rules established
	A clear escalation process and conflict resolution
	Appropriate type and style of review process
	Reward mechanisms for individuals
Team interpersonal relationships	Team working
	Regular communication that is assertive and task focused
	Creating opportunities for giving and receiving feedback
	Open data sources
Inter-team relations	Working across department boundaries
	Input and output across boundaries

JOB ROLES AND RESPONSIBILITIES

Whenever a new team comes together, they are going to go through an emotional journey as they discover their roles and get to know everyone else in the process. To bring this to life, I reference Tuckman's Team Relationship model, which summarises the evolution and non-linear journey that teams go through – forming, norming, storming, performing and adjourning – as they build relationships with each other.[11] The team can go back and forth between norming and storming several times before they reach the performing stage.

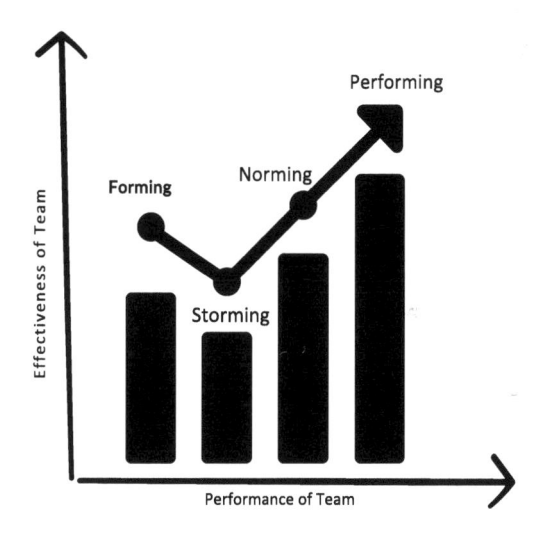

Tuckman's Team and Relationship model

It's good to share this model in one of your first team meetings, so that everyone is aware of the emotional journey they could go on as a team and knows that

---

11 B Tuckman, 'Development sequences in small groups', *Psychological Bulletin*, 63 (1965), 384–99

it's OK to feel negative emotions. It's important that they feel able to discuss the right ways to handle these challenges if they arise.

Forming	Actions: establishing roles, purpose, leadership, ways of working, boundaries etc
	Experiences: polite, watchful, uncertain and impersonal
Storming	Actions: questioning, clarifying or redefining roles, goals, accountabilities
	Experiences: testing, confrontations, debates, discussions
Norming	Actions: establishing norm, questions answered, issues dealt
	Experiences: calming down, structure established, collaboration, working together
Performing	Actions: established structure, continued improvement, consistent performance
	Experiences: change and develop, learn from other mistakes, respond to needs
Adjourning	Actions: project completed and team separates
	Experiences: sense of sadness, accomplishment, anxiety

At the end of this chapter, you should understand how to lay the foundations for a successful project team and to set intentions for how everyone works together to gain the same outcome.

PART FOUR
EVALUATING THE BUSINESS NEED

K
KPIs For Measuring ROI

Your customer asks, 'If I spend £1m on this project, what benefits am I going to get for it?'

As a consultant, do you know how to demonstrate the ROI to secure budget?

If a business is considering investing in Salesforce products, it's important to support any internal teams and external consultancy costs with a clear business case and ROI. Determining the value of a CRM system like Salesforce requires effort but it is necessary to justify expenses as well as ensure successful strategies and business growth.

In this chapter, you'll find out how to calculate the ROI of your project and justify this in your pitch.

WHAT CAN GO WRONG?

If there isn't a clear ROI, it is likely that the CoE and executive sponsor won't invest any more budget in the Salesforce team, product or related activities. Without the right investment, there will be insufficient resources for the team to implement or manage Salesforce effectively. This will cause the project to falter or, worse, be abandoned/the team replaced.

HOW TO GET IT RIGHT

Success means demonstrating the value that Salesforce can bring to the company and team and showing that the cost will be outweighed by the benefits. To ensure there is an ongoing investment in the Salesforce team for salaries, products and resources, you will need to justify its reason for being and the financial contribution it makes to the company's profit margin by improving processes to reduce costs and increase profits.

How to measure improvements

To be able to calculate and demonstrate ROI, you'll need to have ways of identifying and measuring the improvements that result from the Salesforce CRM. To achieve this, you need to:

1. Identify the drivers for organisational and departmental change

2. Define tangible (with a clear monetary value) and intangible benefits (other improvements)

3. Review your current baseline statistics

4. Agree your goals for the future

5. Define SMART (specific, measurable, achievable, realistic, time-framed) measures of success

Below are some example indicators you could use in different areas:

Customer service	Improved feedback score
	Increase in impact and outcomes
	Improved referral rates
Stakeholder engagement	Improved engagement rates
	Increase in ROI in campaigns
	Improved retention rates
Efficiency	Reduced costs
	Achieved quality standards
	Reduced leakage
Business intelligence	Ideas for continual improvement
	New innovations
	Improved marketing proposition
Financial sustainability	Quicker customer conversion
	Increased revenue
	Improved financial assurance

Let's delve into the five main indicator areas in a bit more depth.

Customer service

Has the business invested in Salesforce to improve the customer service experience? To measure the impact it has had, I recommend tracking customer feedback scores to look for potential improvements, such as an increase in repeat customers or referral rates. The better the insights into how your customers respond to your products, services and support, the more likely you are to ensure customer satisfaction in the future.

One easy way to gather these insights is to build and send customer feedback surveys to anyone who has purchased a product from the organisation. When you build customer feedback forms with a Salesforce-integrated data collection platform, each customer response will automatically update the corresponding customer's Salesforce record. This will provide greater visibility of customer satisfaction and will also enable customers to contact your team more easily with any support requests.

Stakeholder engagement rates

If the business has adopted Salesforce to improve customer relationships, it's important that you are accurately capturing contact information and preferences. Once you have engaged with your customers and are communicating to them in their preferred way, you can track any improvement in engagement rates, an increase in ROI of marketing campaigns and, hopefully, improve retention rates.

You can use a Salesforce-integrated data collection platform for clean, accurate data capture into your Salesforce org. With a custom web form, you can easily collect customer information, set browser autocomplete attributes for better prefilling and automatically create or update existing Salesforce records. This data will be up-to-date and easily accessible in Salesforce when contacting stakeholders.

Business efficiency

Does the business plan to use Salesforce to save time and money as well as allocate resources into more profitable activities? Quite often, businesses use automation tools to automatically capture stakeholder information and automate responses to reduce administrative burden. If so, you will benefit from measuring any reduction in costs and time and potentially leakage too.

Again, a Salesforce-integrated data collection platform will provide a user-friendly way to automate data collection processes and integrate seamlessly with Salesforce to minimise wasted resources and team overload. Eliminating manual data entry minimises risk of human error, accelerates processing time and frees up teams to spend more time on the most productive tasks that ultimately increase the business's profit.

Business intelligence

Capturing customer and employee feedback, including their ideas and suggestions, can be a great way to plan future business strategies, product updates, marketing campaigns and more. In addition, with this information you can demonstrate how Salesforce has helped you capture new ideas for continual development or improved market proposition.

To collect this valuable information, you can create a survey that captures data and sends it directly to Salesforce. From there, you'll be able to analyse the level of customer and employee engagement, learn about their needs and make strategic adjustments.

Financial sustainability

Another reason why businesses invest in Salesforce and third-party apps is because they want to convert customers faster. To achieve this, you need the ability to streamline online product purchases while keeping any contact or payment information secure.

A common solution is to create online payment pages. These forms simplify processes where more significant contracts are involved that require e-signature and payment solutions. Implementing such solutions enables you to measure any increase in customer conversion rate and/or speed, increases in revenue and improved financial assurance.

How to estimate costs and ROI

In Chapter A we covered costs related to an actual Salesforce project implementation, but there are other costs you might need to consider for an internal business case – for example, licences for products and other related setup costs, resources for customisation and management, software updates and training.

How to calculate the ROI

Calculating the ROI of the new Salesforce CRM requires you to first estimate then compare the expected cost of development and operation with the benefits of making the change once it's complete.

ROI = expected average annual profit × 100 / total investment

For example: (50,000 / 5) × 100 / 100,000 = 10%

At the end of this chapter, you should be able to mobilise your client to identify the most relevant KPIs to measure and demonstrate the ROI of their digital transformation project, and present a solid business case for continued investment.

Thank you to 360 SMS for sponsoring this chapter. In *Cracking the SMS Conversion Code*, 360 SMS help customers understand the ROI that can be generated through using integrated communication tools and share how companies can grow their revenue.

The 360 SMS App is a communication suite built natively on Salesforce, facilitating customer communications via SMS, WhatsApp, LINE, CTI dialler, Facebook, Instagram and WeChat.

L
Legacy Adoption Issues

Your customer says, 'No one uses Salesforce.'

'Why not?' You ask.

'I don't know,' the customer replies.

As the consultant, do you know how to uncover the truth behind any legacy issues?

In this chapter, you'll find out how to identify the root cause of user adoption issues with our handy assessment methodology.

If you are relaunching a CRM in an organisation that has historically had poor user adoption, it's important to first uncover where the issues arose. From my experience, the root cause is normally in one of six areas.

WHAT CAN GO WRONG?

If you don't uncover legacy issues, then the same barriers to success can re-occur and prevent successful adoption again. You need to figure out where things went wrong previously and to get to the truth so that you can understand and then fix the problem.

HOW TO GET IT RIGHT

Returning to the NLP Logical Levels model that I referred to in Chapter E, which explores where issues or pain points can arise in a situation, this same model can be repositioned and easily applied to a legacy Salesforce project.

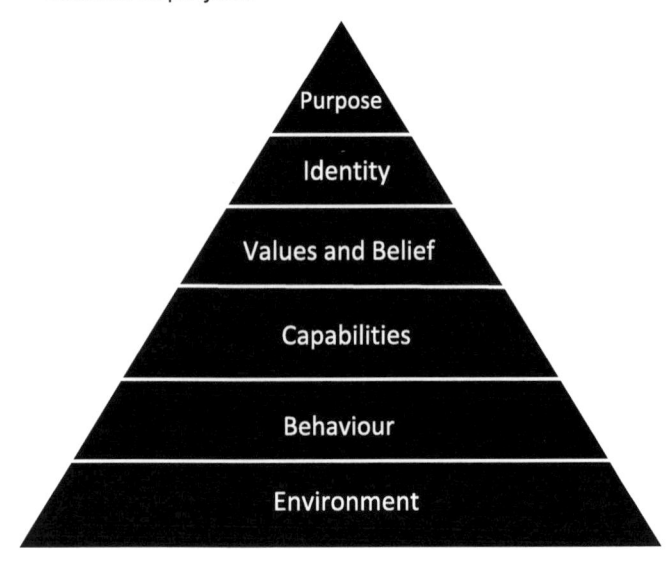

NLP Logical Levels

Finding the root cause

Below are six areas to explore with your executive sponsor and CoE team to get to the root of legacy issues and the reasons for past failures. It can also be beneficial to have exploratory conversations with different teams and departments to get a holistic perspective and overall view of the organisation. From my experience, the opinions and attitudes of end users working on the ground can be quite different to those of the management team. A series of discovery workshops is useful as part of a health check (see Chapter O next). Once you have uncovered the area(s) that are influencing adoption, you can then create a strategy to resolve the issues.

Purpose

How do the management perceive Salesforce as transforming the delivery and performance of their organisation? Are they bought into its higher purpose? Ideally, they should want Salesforce to fundamentally change the way their company does business and serves their customers, for the better. If they aren't bought into a solid business case that showcases digital transformation, then this is the vision that needs consolidating to make the new project a success.

Identity

Are the management team using Salesforce to manage performance? How are staff responding to the introduction or adoption of Salesforce? They need to believe that Salesforce will be central to their world and that they can't live without it. It has to be the heart of the organisation and they should relish in the idea of real-time performance analysis and everyday business use. If they see it as a sideline data admin tool that they 'should' use but don't have to or need to, this is the problem you need to solve.

Beliefs/values

What do different teams/departments feel that Salesforce offers them in terms of value and benefits? Are the managers and end users bought into using it? If teams don't know or perceive the benefits to the business and to their role, this could be the root of the adoption issue.

Capabilities

How confident are users in using Salesforce currently? Has the training that's been done given users adequate skills and confidence? Has the Salesforce administrator been given sufficient resources to manage the system and users? It might be that users simply need additional training and/or support to use the system and more needs to be invested in Salesforce admin support to resolve the low adoption issues.

Behaviour

Are people consistently using Salesforce in the same way? Have clear rules and processes been mapped out for how they *should* use Salesforce? Has there been any investment in BA? If there are no clear business rules or processes for when and how to use Salesforce, then people won't use the system consistently, or at all – this is the source of your adoption problem.

Environment

Can people access the system via a user-friendly interface, regardless of whether they are working from a laptop, mobile or tablet? Do they need to upload data, either on- or offline? Is Salesforce well integrated with other technical systems or are there data silos and clunky systems?

If people are having to work around different systems and can't easily access what they need, this is going to affect user adoption. Technical integration or replacement might be the solution to this problem, along with a good UX design.

Data integrity

I'm going to throw a seventh area on the table, one that isn't represented in the NLP Logical Levels, but is important in the context of legacy/adoption issues – poor data integrity. From what I've seen, in many legacy projects one of the biggest reasons users do not adopt CRMs, including Salesforce, is because they don't trust the data. Poor data governance can impact the organisation significantly; for example:[12]

- Inaccurate or incomplete data can lead to productivity stalling by as much as 20%, the equivalent of one working day of work each week.
- The average company loses 12% of its revenue as a result of inaccurate data.
- 40% of all business initiatives fail to deliver their targeted benefits because of poor-quality data.

To avoid the above issues, you will need to work with the client to understand exactly what good data integrity looks like. The first step is to understand how data is used by the organisation and what data is most important to driving business performance and intelligence. A data governance plan should be created and governed by a steering group that owns the responsibility for data integrity.

Once you understand what data is most important to the business, you need to determine your quality data

---

12 'Introduction to data governance and stewardship: Best practices to improve the quality of your customer data', Salesforce (2016), https://a.sfdcstatic.com/content/dam/www/ocms-backup/assets/pdf/misc/data_Governance_Stewardship_ebook.pdf, accessed August 2023

LEGACY ADOPTION ISSUES

indicators and assess the quality of the data as it currently stands in the system.

We have a free Health Check Template download that you can use to carry out a data integrity analysis. Validity also offer a suite of data integrity tools to quickly clean and manage Salesforce data. All of these are available via the book resources page here:

[QR code: SCAN ME]

With this chapter, you have a structured approach to assess the root cause(s) of any legacy user adoption issues and can propose solutions to prevent the same issues from reoccurring when you relaunch the CRM. Quite often, the resolution is found in winning over hearts and minds via the right communication rather than in any functionality of the tech.

Thank you to Validity for sponsoring this chapter. DemandTools by Validity is a secure data quality platform that enables organisations to clean and manage Salesforce data quickly, enabling everyone to do their jobs more effectively, efficiently and profitably.

M
Mentoring

> Your customer asks, 'What is expected of me and when on this project?'
>
> *As a consultant, do you know how best to support your new users during the design, testing and roll-out?*

Your role as a Salesforce consultant could entail mentoring the executive sponsor, CoE members, a Salesforce technical team or the end users you are training throughout the project life cycle.

As the Salesforce consultant, you must be a trusted adviser. Personally, I have felt privileged to work with senior managers who put their trust in me, to guide them and their teams to success on a CRM project, which is quite often an entirely new experience for many and a transformational change for the whole business and employees. It's no small task.

It is good to frame your relationship as a mentoring relationship, so your client knows you are there to support them on their learning journey. In this chapter, we look at how you can create the foundations of a strong mentoring relationship with your stakeholders.

WHAT CAN GO WRONG?

> If you don't establish trust, build rapport and implement a framework for working with people, then the relationship can fall apart. Implementing a Salesforce project requires a lot of effort and energy from various different stakeholders, and everyone is on a learning journey. If you don't teach them the why, how, what and when, they won't know what to do, leading to frustration and upset.

HOW TO GET IT RIGHT

> A mentoring relationship can take different forms depending on who is involved, so it's important to carefully consider your approach and tailor it depending on the circumstances you find yourself in.

How to be a mentor

Great mentors are motivated to build and nurture mentoring relationships. Anyone can be a mentor, but in my experience there are ten specific qualities that make mentors exceptional:

- **Reliability** – an exceptional mentor is trustworthy, consistent, and dependable.

- **Persistence** – an exceptional mentor is persistent.

- **Respect** – an exceptional mentor respects their mentee. They see their mentee's positive attributes and achievements. They honour their mentee's beliefs, opinions, background, and choices. In order for a mentoring relationship to have a real lasting impact it must be based on mutual respect.

- **Humour** – an exceptional mentor has a good sense of humour. We can often be too hard on ourselves. It is the role of mentor to be flexible, to know when to be silly and when to be serious. At times, the mentee may find it hard to see the funny side. Like any other tool, humour, when used appropriately, can help shift the mentee's perspective and energy, from stuck to unstuck.

- **Patience** – an exceptional mentor understands that each mentee will take a different amount of time to learn and understand something. It is important to have patience, knowing when to push your mentee and when to give them space and time.

- **Intuition** – an exceptional mentor knows how to harness his or her intuition for the benefit of the mentee. A mentor needs to be wary of always relying only on conscious reasoning. Intuition is an incredibly powerful tool, more powerful than logic.

- **Curiosity** – an exceptional mentor is curious about the mentee's thoughts. Using curiosity, intuition and powerful questions, a mentor does not make assumptions, but instead gains an honest understanding of who the mentee is and what they want.

- **Honesty** – an exceptional mentor is honest about who they are and what they are capable of, as well as what they notice in their mentee. Being truthful is incredibly important because it supports a relationship based on trust. Nonetheless, truth should never be wielded in a malicious, intentionally hurtful manner.

- **Self-regulation** – an exceptional mentor knows how to regulate his or her own emotions in a mentoring session. As a mentor, your state of mind and your body language have an impact on the mentoring relationship. Make sure to leave your personal and professional issues outside the mentoring session. How will you know if you are not self-regulating? You may start to daydream, talk to yourself, get angry and/or apathetic.

- **Commitment** – an exceptional mentor is committed to their mentee. Your role as a mentor is very important. Make sure you understand the level of time and energy commitment that mentoring requires before you agree to such a relationship.

The mentoring relationship

To build a strong mentoring relationship, the mentor and mentee should collaborate on the following areas:

- **Agree SMART outcomes and goals**: specific, measurable, achievable, realistic and time-framed.

- **Understanding learning styles.** Learning styles are different approaches to or ways of learning, based on individuals' preferred ways of interacting with, absorbing and processing information. There are four main learning styles – visual, auditory, read/write and kinaesthetic – which we'll return to later. For most people, one learning style dominates, although some individuals have a balance between all of them. Search for a VAK (Visual, Auditory, and Kinesthetic) test online. Once you know your mentee's preferred learning style(s), you can tailor your communication to suit them.

- **Creating a mentoring plan.** Agree how, when and where you will be meeting. Make it a routine so there is accountability regarding outcomes and goals. Of course, if something suddenly comes up that they need support with, that's OK too, but agree the boundaries for communication between meetings – eg phone calls or emails – so you both know what is reasonable.

- **Creating a mentoring agreement.** The purpose of the agreement is to create a safe space for the mentee in which they can be vulnerable; establish the mentee's trust; help the mentor know how to work with the mentee in an empowering manner that empowers the mentee; and to determine how the mentor and mentee will engage.

- **Recognising and handling barriers.** All relationships come with barriers that, when not addressed, can lead to the breakdown of the relationship. When these barriers are identified, it might be helpful to unpack what is actually going on for the mentee. For example, focusing on a technical requirement might create a barrier if their confidence has taken a hit or they're struggling with imposter syndrome.

What are mentoring skills?

There are various skills that one needs to possess or acquire in order to be a good mentor. In my experience, the key ones are:

- **Effective listening** – as a mentor, one of your most important roles is to listen. You must be able to hear what your mentee is and is not saying. Humans can listen in a variety of different ways, some of which are more effective in a mentoring environment than others.

- **Effective questioning** – generally, we know that asking questions is good for learning, but the type of questions we ask and how we phrase them will make a big difference to what kind and quality of response we get. A good mentor knows how to ask questions that will elicit a useful answer or insight.

- **Action planning** – one of the qualities that distinguishes mentoring from other similar relationships is the emphasis on the mentee's action. For the mentee, this is about achieving outcomes. It's all very well setting SMART goals but if there are no action steps to reach the goal, it remains a dream. That's why one of the key skills of a mentor is action planning.

- **Providing feedback** – feedback in mentoring is a two-way process and should be built into the initial coaching agreement, where both the mentee and mentor have permission to give each other feedback. Between them, they can agree on when to give feedback and how to structure it as part of the mentoring relationship.

- **Giving guidance versus advice** – circumstances are important here. If you are acting as the trusted adviser on a project, you will be imparting advice as a mentor. If you are teaching people how to use Salesforce, you might want to progress from an official advisory role to a position of guidance, with a view to your mentee becoming self-sufficient and empowered to come up with their own solutions rather than rely on your advice.

In summary, my three top tips for a successful mentoring relationship would be:

1. Agree the goals and outcomes
2. Create a comprehensive and structured mentoring plan
3. Identify your mentee's learning style and tailor the way you communicate with them

If you want to learn more about mentoring and practise your mentoring skills, you can sign up to be a volunteer mentor with Supermums and work with our new trainees. Find out more on the book resources page.

At the end of this chapter, you should feel equipped to build effective mentoring relationships with stakeholders by understanding their learning style and agreeing a plan with clear objectives and outcomes, so that everyone is set up for achieving a great end result.

N
Navigating Stakeholders

> The end users say, 'Why are we making changes to systems and processes?'
>
> *As a consultant, do you know how to influence different stakeholders in the right way to engage and enthuse them?*

In this chapter, we introduce some more change management concepts and learn about different organisational cultures, how you can adapt your management style when needed and how to carry out stakeholder mapping to understand which camp people are sitting in emotionally.

Effectively navigating stakeholders is the glue holding your Salesforce project together. Knowing how to communicate in a variety of ways is intrinsic to a successful approach to BA and Agile PM, yet this discipline is too often overlooked by Salesforce professionals.

If you don't understand the culture of the organisation or the feelings of your stakeholders, it's likely that your communication and change management strategy will be off kilter, resulting in your stakeholders disengaging with the Salesforce system.

WHAT CAN GO WRONG?

There are many failures in navigating stakeholders that can ultimately lead to project failure. In my experience, the big ones are:

- Stakeholders not being bought into a new system or changing their processes
- Tasks not being completed as expected
- Stakeholders ignoring requests for information
- People not showing up for meetings

HOW TO GET IT RIGHT

To navigate stakeholders well, you need to understand the organisation's culture and to tailor your approach accordingly.

Organisational culture

To understand organisational culture and how this affects the way you navigate your engagement of and with stakeholders, I find Gareth Morgan's organisational metaphors[13] helpful – see these in the table below. You also want to look at the different emotional states that your stakeholders might be in. What is their level of energy and commitment? Cameron and Green organise people into four different camps in this regard, as shown in the below image, and provide some example strategies you can adopt with each.[14]

	'Blocker'	'Champions'
High Energy	Can obstruct or prevent the change happening. Strategy: reduce their power and energy.	Advocate and active implementers of change. Strategy: Keep them fully involved and maintain momentum.
Low Energy	'Sleepers' Not bothered about change or not aware of it. Strategy: Wake them up and establish their interest in the change.	'Preachers' In positions of power whose opinion counts but don't consider change a priority. Strategy: Keep informed and focused on the change.
	Low Energy	**High**

Cameron and Green's stakeholder categorisation

I've worked on projects with organisations that represent all of these different cultures, and adopted all

---

13 G Morgan, *Images of Organization* (Sage Publications, 1986)
14 E Cameron and M Green, *Making Sense of Change Management*, 2nd edition (Kogan Page, 2009)

of these approaches. It's important to recognise and respect the culture of the organisation you are working for and to discuss the different techniques with the executive sponsor and CoE to ensure they adopt the approach that best aligns to their culture. There are risks with all of these approaches, so a blended methodology could also be proposed to the client in some cases.

Approach/ metaphor	Culture in practice	Consultancy techniques
Top-down ('machine' culture)	Senior management drives change	Training is provided
	Targets and timescales specified	Consultants advise on approach
	Resistance can be managed	
Representation ('political system' culture)	Influential person initiates change	Champion group of stakeholders
	Representation of views	Input of expertise and influence
		New ways of working deployed
Collaboration ('organism' culture)	Led by HR/improvement/OPs team	Research techniques
	Awareness of a need for change	Stakeholder participation
		Co-design solutions

Approach/ metaphor	Culture in practice	Consultancy techniques
Bottom-up ('flux and transformation' culture)	Change is initiated from the grass-roots	Collective discussion forums
	Management figures facilitates process	Plan emerges from discussions
		Plan is presented to authority for acceptance

It's a useful exercise to analyse who within the organisation falls where; you can either do this yourself or working with the management team. You will want to apply a different strategy for communicating with and motivating people depending on what segment they're in. We'll look at some different motivational strategies in Chapter S.

At the end of this chapter, you should be able to identify the culture of the organisation you're working in and the emotions of your stakeholders so you can plan a communication strategy accordingly to engage different types of stakeholder.

Thank you to MarCloud for sponsoring this chapter. MarCloud is a leading marketing automation consultancy and Salesforce partner specialising in Pardot, Marketing Cloud and Salesforce CRM. They are experts in enabling businesses to implement communication strategies using marketing automation tools. Their mission is to bring together the most passionate and competent Salesforce marketing professionals in the space to make businesses more competitive through effective use of the entire Marketing Cloud and Salesforce CRM.

O
Org Analysis

> The consultant says, 'What has been done to this Salesforce system before?'
>
> *As a consultant, do you know how to appraise an existing Salesforce system to uncover the how, what and why of an existing system?*

In this chapter, you'll find out how to carry out org analysis and run a health check. I'll also provide a downloadable template and some recommendations for free org analysis products.

As the Salesforce ecosystem has matured, so has each customer's use of the platform, adding complexity, new functionality and challenges. This means that, as a consultant, chances are you'll be tasked with digging into existing orgs more often than setting up net new implementations. I covered how to discover legacy issues in Chapter L, and this is useful supplement to an org analysis to uncover the roots of user adoption issues.

If you find yourself inheriting an existing Salesforce system, there will always be an initial fear about what you will find when you look under the hood. For example, did you know that, on average, each Salesforce org has over 24,000 metadata items to manage?[15] That means if you click on each setup item and review it for five seconds, it would take you more than four days to review everything in the org.

As a consultant, however much I preferred to work on brand-new greenfield implementations, I inevitably had a good handful of legacy systems that needed a reboot, and I needed a formula and process for conducting this type of audit. It can feel like quite an accomplishment to successfully pivot a failure into a success.

WHAT CAN GO WRONG?

> If you don't conduct a proper org analysis and health check, you won't have the foundational knowledge of the system you need to be able prioritise or make changes to an existing system. Making changes to an org without an understanding of its setup could have repercussions for other development work and existing users' functionality. There is a recipe to follow and specific ingredients that need to be put into the mix to produce the right outcome.

---

15 Hubbl Benchmark Report 2023, www.hubbl.com/campaign/benchmark-report-2023, accessed August 2023

ORG ANALYSIS

HOW TO GET IT RIGHT

In the overall appraisal of an existing org and review of legacy issues, it is important to go through a BA cycle and understand their current business needs. This is to assess how well the system is performing functionally and technically against these needs, achieved through a series of audits. I call this process a health check.

On our Supermums Consultancy Skills course we deliver a session on how to conduct a health check on an existing Salesforce org and share a free health check template; you can download the template from the book resources page.

How to conduct a health check on your Salesforce org

1. Complete an initial BA consultation

Initially, you want to understand the nature of the organisation and the original objectives and motivations for implementing the CRM. You will also need to establish what progress has been made towards these goals and the perceived challenges and successes to date. This will enable you to establish priorities for the health check and review.

To achieve this, you will need to conduct a BA exercise with the executive sponsor and with different departments to understand their services, current business priorities, drivers and motivations for using the CRM.

2. Product and user adoption review

Once you've completed the BA, the next stage is to carry out a technical audit of the system, particularly relating to user adoption. You first need to ask and understand the criteria for good user adoption and then implement checks and balances by installing a user adoption dashboard, if there isn't already one set up. For guidance on this, see Chapter U – User Adoption.

Then you'll need to assess which Salesforce products people are using with a detailed review of which features they are using for each product. This helps you to assess if they are making the most of the product features, whether they are aware of them of all and whether they could glean more value from adopting more features.

Since Salesforce metadata is well structured, I recommend taking advantage of automated audit tools like Hubbl Diagnostics to help simplify current state diagnosis. For example, look for tools that help you review the utilisation of each object, organised by Salesforce Cloud. This will help you to complete the product and feature review section of the health check template linked to above. Automatically identifying native capabilities that users are not currently leveraging will enable you to be more efficient with your time and drive more value for your customers.

3. System governance and management review

It's useful to talk through what a great governance framework looks like with the client and to check what they already have in place. For example, do they have a CoE? A Salesforce champion group? A Salesforce technical team? Who is responsible for delivering on the four roles of a Salesforce admin to manage the system?

As part of the system appraisal, you will want to mobilise several reports, including the Salesforce optimiser report, security health check report, NPSP health check report and error handling. You'll also want to automate the Well-Architected review of your org. This can help uncover issues and recommendations for remediation. Salesforce recently released the Well-Architected framework to help drive customers to build more trusted, easy-to-use and adaptable solutions. I highly recommend you familiarise yourself with this content as it can help guide customers towards better overall success.

4. Data governance and management review

At this step of the health check, you need first to understand what data is valuable for the organisation for business objectives. For example, how does the organisation use data to drive decisions, market activities and serve customers? Once you know which data fields are important, you can then conduct an audit on the quality of data within these fields.

I would also recommend you install a data quality app from the AppExchange and a complementary management tool. Once you have reviewed the quality of data, you can then make recommendations for improving the management of data integrity in the future and create a plan for cleansing any data as needed.

I always recommend using pre-built solutions versus custom, which means leveraging the right tools to help you deliver value to your customers faster. I recently came across Hubbl Diagnostics, a free solution that provides a comprehensive overview into any Salesforce org. It aligns your customer's org to the Well-Architected framework while providing executive-level visualisations to walk your customer through the state of their org. Inevitably, customers will ask how their org compares to others in the ecosystem. Previously, this was near impossible to answer. Now, with this free diagnostics tool, you can get a quantitative, objective understanding of where the org stands compared to the wider ecosystem, while gleaning machine learning-derived insights about what to do next.

The free app can be downloaded from the book resources page:

At the end of this chapter, you should be fully equipped with various tools and templates you can use to carry out an org analysis and health check. This will enable you to understand the current situation of the Salesforce org and to prioritise and plan a list of deliverables to be executed.

> Thank you to Hubbl Diagnostics for sponsoring this chapter. Hubbl Diagnostics are on a mission to uplift and empower the Salesforce ecosystem through powerful org intelligence. Their solution provides admins, architects and consultants with broad and actionable insights into any Salesforce org. Their proprietary metadata aggregation also provides benchmark data to easily measure and compare org complexity against others in your industry.

P
Project Tools

> Your customer says, 'Where was that document again?'
>
> *As a consultant, how do you store, collaborate and communicate on projects?*

In this chapter, we discuss which tools and systems you need to have in place to manage your project and communicate with your stakeholders successfully.

I've counted up to seventy tasks that need to be completed on any one project, depending on whether you are working as an internal or external consultant. There are a lot of common tasks across each project and, as the consultant, you need to manage these properly so that you don't lose or forget things. These typical project tasks will range from marketing, security, deliverables to system licence setup and deactivation. Within each of these project tasks there needs to be a way to document, communicate, share files and collaborate with project stakeholders.

WHAT CAN GO WRONG?

If you don't have the right project tools and systems in place, the following circumstances can arise:

- Tasks don't get completed as there is no reminder or clear deadline, resulting in project delays.
- Information related to a project gets lost in emails that have been shared, which impacts the build.
- Compliance is not followed as data sharing isn't secure.
- Emails are not getting answered as they get shunted out of sight by new incoming emails.
- Clients prefer to use their own tools, meaning you end up working across multiple systems.

HOW TO GET IT RIGHT

Having the right project tools can be a game changer for co-ordination and producing effective collaboration and communication with a client on a project.

As part of our Supermums Consultancy Skills training programme, I deliver a module called the Salesforce Consultant Toolkit, which provides an essential set of tools to ensure your project is a success. I also talk through the seventy tasks to complete during the project life cycle and how to manage all of them.

PROJECT TOOLS

With so many tasks involved, having tools/systems in place to coordinate efforts is essential. In my experience, there are five main tools required.

- A **project management** tool is needed to track tasks and utilisation of time and budget against the project deliverables.
- A **user requirements** solution will enable you to log all of the functional/non-functional requirements and the associated technical requirements that need to be built for the system.
- **Communication tool** – ideally, this should be integrated with your other tools, giving the ability to converse back and forth on project tasks and requirements.
- You need a **file-sharing solution** where clients can share information with the Salesforce team to avoid things getting lost in emails. It also gives you a single source of truth, where you should store everything.
- Use **process mapping software** to map out before and after processes and produce documents such as object entity diagrams.

PM tools

When I was researching this topic, I couldn't find a 'perfect' project management solution amongst the Salesforce Ohana. Quite often, I'd be recommended two different tools for internal project and resource management compared to ones for liaising with clients on project deliverables. There is debate about how often clients might want to log into a system, which is dependent on the client's preference and size of project. Integrations were also common, allowing people to build a fully rounded solution – Asana with Slack, for example

Nevertheless, some of the most commonly cited products were:

- Jira and Confluence
- Asana (with Slack and Flowsana)
- Taskray
- Trello
- Experience Cloud with a third-party app

To illustrate some of their relative strengths and weaknesses, below are some comments from the community:

> 'We use mission control for the internal management of our projects, milestones, budget and resources planning and time log monitoring. We use Jira (open to our clients) to build the solution. Both tools work fine but I still find that we have a gap with the organisation of the project tasks that are not part of the solution build. We have not settled yet on a specific tool for this.'

> 'We use Task Ray to collaborate with our Salesforce partners and internal data team.

We use Asana for broader collaboration with our internal team and stakeholders, who are often not heavy Salesforce users but depend on the outcomes of our projects. PM often involves a combination of several platforms, though. Either way, our PM and planning relies on a good mix of visualisation and planning tools like Miro, LucidChart and Google Sheets when we need it.'

'We use Jira with focused Confluence pages to keep current priorities and in-progress work easily accessible to the stakeholder.'

'I've been using Asana lately, with Flowsana for automating things like assigning and form submission for client tickets. It had a lot of integrations – I especially like the Slack integration because you can just reply to clients right from Slack but it's all synced back to Asana.'[16]

By the end of this chapter, you should be more informed about the array of different project tools that can help set you and your stakeholders up for success when working on a project. It's always worth asking people for their feedback and recommendations, getting demonstrations and finding a tool that works for you as well as customers.

---

16 Black, H, *How to project manage Salesforce projects* (Supermums, 2021), https://supermums.org/how-to-project-manage-salesforce-projects/, accessed 4 September 2023

PART FIVE
PREPARING FOR ROLL-OUT

Q
Quality Testing

The consultant says, 'Why isn't this working?'

As a consultant, don't forget to test your work yourself before it's rolled out for user testing.

For this chapter, I'm delighted to have had a guest contributor – Sydnie Mulcahy, the content lead at Provar Testing – provide expert guidance on how to choose the right test automation tool.

WHAT CAN GO WRONG?

> If you don't do your own quality testing before user testing, and there are errors, it will be highly embarrassing when you have to try and uncover and resolve (if you can) the issue in the middle of a testing session. I think we have all been there, but it's best to try and avoid it if you can.

HOW TO GET IT RIGHT

It is a highly recommended that you test the Salesforce system before roll-out into production and before user testing, to ensure it's working as expected. There are two stages to quality testing: technical testing, where you assess if the product is working effectively without errors; and functional testing, where you assess if the product is fit for purpose and your end users. If you're ready to take the next step in your Salesforce testing journey, you may want to considering adding a test automation tool to your workflow.

Test automation

With myriad options available, selecting the right tool for your team's needs can be a daunting task. There are many aspects to consider before making your selection, and every test automation tool has its benefits and drawbacks. They all provide different levels of ease of use, training, scalability, future-proofing, security, level of support, pricing and more, but how do you know what factors will make or break your team's strategy?

This will depend on the size and scale of your team, as well as what stage of the testing journey you are at. If you're just getting started with manual testing, for instance, you may prioritise a vendor with stellar post-sale support and training to get you up and running, but if you're well into automated testing already, it may be more helpful to look for a solution that makes your existing tests more efficient, saving you time and money.

The process of evaluating a testing tool or solution can be simplified into seven key areas, as follows:

1. Test resilience or fragility
2. Polymorphism and reusability
3. Ease of use and learning
4. Testing adjacent systems
5. Support
6. Training
7. Customer success

Below is a rundown of what to look for in each category and some suggested questions and demo requests you can put to the vendor.

Test resilience or fragility

This concerns to what degree updates to the Salesforce system or updates to customisations are likely to break tests and cause rework.

Salesforce updates its platform multiple times per year, which can cause automated tests to break unless your testing tool was designed to operate with Salesforce. Between Salesforce updates, changes to customisations can also cause automated tests to break. Tests that break lead to reworks, higher costs and other negative consequences.

Here are some demos to request during your evaluation to test this area:

- Build a simple customisation to create an opportunity.
- Create a test script that tests that the opportunity has been successfully created.
- Make changes to the page layout, such as adding fields or changing the location of the fields on the page, and run the test case again.
- Create a test and show me how it continues to work when you move a button on the layout, for example.
- Show me, step by step, how your testing solution handles shadow DOM[17] elements.

Polymorphism and reusability

To what extent does the solution adapt to the needs of the rest of the organisation by utilising a single test that can run across numerous contexts?

---

17   Document Object Model

QUALITY TESTING

The technology that makes tests resilient also enables polymorphism (where one test can run across numerous contexts) and reusability. Polymorphic tests that are reusable across your workflow reduce the time, effort and expense of creating and maintaining tests. Fewer tests with more coverage mean a higher-quality solution that can evolve more quickly and easily.

Below is a demo to request during your evaluation to test this area:

> 'Using the test from the prior demo (test resiliency), run that same test in a different environment (eg, validation versus development) in a different language (eg, French), on a different browser, for a different user profile (eg, a marketing VP/director) with special permissions (eg, that reveal sensitive data like total bookings companywide).'

Ease of use and learning

What skills and experience levels are required to create, maintain, and run tests?

Many people involved in Salesforce customisations are considered 'citizen developers' – folks who may not necessarily be experts in programming languages and frameworks. It is important that the skills required to test Salesforce customisations are similar to the citizen developer skills needed to create the customisation, so that these testers can easily work with their counterparts as they participate in, or even fully own, the testing process.

Here are some ways to test this area in your evaluation:

- Build a test case with the solution to see how easy and intuitive it is.
- Try to interact with the test case in real-time: add, delete, update steps, pause, rewind etc.
- Run a test script for a test that needs to be debugged and see if it passes/fails in real-time or if you must run the test over again once it is fixed to confirm the issue is resolved.

Testing adjacent systems

To what extent is the system capable of running end-to-end tests that reach adjacent non-Salesforce systems?

Every Salesforce platform connects to other enterprise systems and custom integration points, and it's important that a Salesforce testing solution can reach out to other systems and test workflows end to end.

Here is a demo to request during your evaluation to test this area:

> 'Test an end-to-end scenario such as email to case, website lead to Salesforce, lead to cash, etc.'

Support

To what degree does a vendor offer ongoing support through demonstrations, one-on-one consultations, online help centres, trade show presence etc?

The level of ongoing support a vendor provides their customers after closing the sale is essential to consider. This support can come in a number of verticals: demos, one-on-one consultations, online help centres and community forums, a consistent trade show presence and more. The more willing a vendor is to help their customers in the long run, the stronger the relationship will become and the more trust you can have in the product, leading to greater overall satisfaction.

Here are some questions you can ask during your evaluation to test this area:

- After the initial setup consultation, how do you provide continued support to your customers?
- Do you have an easily accessible online help centre or a community forum?
- How quickly will I be able to connect with an expert from your team with questions, and what hours are you available?
- Are you attending any upcoming trade shows or conferences in my area?

Training

Whether or not a vendor offers additional or ongoing training services beyond the initial consultation or setup is another important consideration.

A good vendor will prioritise continued education. As product updates are made and new features are introduced, vendors should offer readily accessible courses that users can take in their own time to brush up their skills. They can also offer continued training through webinars, blog posts and white papers.

Here are some questions you can ask during your evaluation to test this area:

- Do you offer training courses for users to expand their product knowledge?
- Do you offer free webinars for customers?
- Do you have a blog?
- Do you have a library of white papers available for browsing?

Customer success

The best indication of whether a vendor is the right fit for your team is their customer success stories. Look

QUALITY TESTING

for the number of customers who have shared positive accounts of using the vendor's products (and also make note of any negative feedback), and spend time gauging the calibre of reviews from reputable industry review sites, peers and analysts.

Here are some questions you can ask during your evaluation to test this area:

- Do you have customer case studies or success stories available from within our industry?

- When I was researching your company, I noticed that there was negative feedback published on [site] regarding [topic]. Can you speak to this feedback, such as ways your company has improved this area of business?

- Do you have any reviews you could provide from reputable industry review sites, peers and/or analysts?

- Would any of your existing or past customers be willing to answer a few questions?

By the end of this chapter, you should be more informed about what quality testing is, why it's important, what an automated testing tool can offer you and how to go about selecting the tool that is right for your project or organisation.

Thank you to Provar for sponsoring this chapter. Provar were the first Salesforce testing app and can transform your testing experience, saving you time and costs, accelerating your delivery and catching bugs before they disrupt users. Globally, they operate out of the UK, USA and India and with over a hundred employees and forty partners, they are a trusted app worldwide.

R
Running A Great Product Demo

The customer says, 'I'm struggling to visualise what Salesforce can do for us.'

As a consultant, do you know how to deliver a great demo for your stakeholders?

In this chapter find out how to develop and perfect your demo to wow your audience and get them bought into using Salesforce.

Being able to deliver a great product demo is a key skill for a consultant and is required for both BA and change management. You will need to deliver demos throughout the project life cycle, from pre-customer sales engagement through to design workshops, user testing through to end-user training. The ultimate goal of any Salesforce professional is to get users enthused, excited and engaged with new technology at every stage of the journey.

Creating a tailored demo is an important part of this process, as it enables your audience to visualise how the solution will help them achieve their goals. It also gives you the opportunity to showcase and sell Salesforce to your audience, sometimes for the first time. During the demo you will show and explain the range of features that are available to the customer, so they know the possibilities. Often, they don't know want they need or want until you show them what's possible.

In this chapter I talk through the best practice principles of running a great demo so you can wow your audiences and get them excited about using the new technology.

WHAT CAN GO WRONG?

> People make up their minds based on first impressions, and running a demo is your chance to make a great first impression. You want to impress them by speaking their language, making it feel like their brand and showing them that the product is going to meet their needs. If you deliver a demo that is not aligned to their needs, is not structured or, in the worst case, is not working properly, people are going to lose trust in you and lose confidence in what you can deliver.

HOW TO GET IT RIGHT

To perfect your demo style, we are going to run through how to script it, how to set it up from a technical perspective and how to communicate and deliver your demo for success.

Preparing your demo script

You'll need to participate in a discovery exercise before you prepare the demo to elicit the audience's pain points and high-level functional needs so you can tailor the demo. Through this exercise, you want to:

- Identify the pain points for the executives, senior management and front-line team
- Identify the functional requirements that could help solve these pain points
- Map out the proposed solutions so you can prepare a script that speaks to the pain points

Then, identify different personas and create a personalised walk-through of the system to align with different members of your audience.

The script should include an introduction about why you are all in the room, so talk about what you are going to show during the demo – eg, a solution that can improve sales performance or customer service – and the reason why this solution is needed. In doing so, you reinforce their goals and pain points upfront. These pain points might be overarching for the business as a whole, or specific to teams and managers.

For example:

'We can help you solve XYZ pain points through improving ABC functional requirements using the following technology. In this demo, I'm going to show you how.'

You also need an introduction to Salesforce as a company and a product. Talk about its size, reputation, the suite of products it offers and the success stories of similar 'competitors'. Provide examples of how the Salesforce products solve their pain points.

As you go through the demo, keep focused on high-level requirements – don't go into detailed functionality, but reinforce the features that will drive the ROI throughout the script narrative – eg, introducing e-signature contracts to speed up sales conversion.

How to communicate with different types of stakeholders

When delivering the script, you need to have an understanding of how to communicate with and engage stakeholders with different learning styles, as people will see and hear things differently. There are four main learning styles, and individuals typically have a primary and secondary learning style. We will explore learning styles in more depth in Chapter T, but for now, the different learning styles are:

- Kinaesthetic: these learners like to feel how something works and experience how it will meet their needs. They often like to 'have a go'.

- Visual: these learners like to see what the thing they're learning about looks like and how it aligns with their needs, brand and content.

- Read/write: these learners will want to know the details of the solution and service provider. You should include information about the scale of Salesforce, evidence of ROI and so on within your demo to support your narrative.

- Auditory: these learners like to hear stories similar to their own. You should reference successful case studies in similar projects or industries to back up your script.

When you are running a demo, you are effectively selling a solution to people, so check out some additional tips of how to engage your audience in Chapter S.

Technical setup

In regard to the technical components of a demo, you want to keep it simple, to the point and focused on the primary features. You don't want to overwhelm or distract listeners. When preparing the technical elements of your demo, you should:

- Add data that gives personalised touches to the client – eg accounts or products that relate to their story
- Create records and data throughout to tell the customer story
- Remove any fields/related lists that are not relevant to the demo
- Create a personalised app with the company logo
- Show relevant records with accurate data
- Show dashboards populated with data that show positive progress towards ROI objectives using Salesforce – eg sales performance increasing over a three-year period

Delivering a great demo

You want the delivery of your demo to be smooth, structured and efficient. Practise your demo before you take it to your audience, preferably with someone who can give you feedback. You will often need to record a demo and share it with stakeholders as well, so rehearse and practise recording it.

Take a presentation skills course if you are not confident with public speaking. Some top tips for your delivery include:

- Have tabs open in a browser to speed up the demo where relevant – but don't jump through the journey
- Explain Salesforce terminology or change terminology – eg Kanban view/objects
- Demo how to change records and show how that will update dashboard graphs
- Show how you can create/adjust/add to records easily, eg by adding tasks
- Click through from records/list views into records to progress your story
- Show dashboards that speak to exec level
- Wrap up with the ROI

At the end of this chapter, you should have a game plan for preparing and delivering a great product demo. Creating a good demo does take time and effort but it's worth it in terms of optimising end-user buy-in and adoption. If you have ready-prepared sales demos for each type of product you typically use, it should just mean making a few tweaks each time you deliver it. If you are preparing a demo for a newly built CRM system, then this is something you need to build into your time scales and budget.

Thank you to SharinPix for sponsoring this chapter. SharinPix is the proud winner of many App Demo Jams that showcase their product.

SharinPix enables pro photo usage for your users by giving you access to a business-oriented image toolbox and unlimited photo storage at a fixed cost. This toolbox enables you to access all the image features you've ever dreamed of plus various components to build the perfect user experience. This means you no longer need to leave Salesforce to edit, resize, annotate or watermark images. You can also work offline from your mobile device to snap pictures, dictate comments, scan docs and fill in offline forms based on a PDF.

S
Selling Salesforce

> The customer says, 'Why should I use Salesforce?'
>
> *As a consultant, do you know how to sell Salesforce to your users?*

In this chapter, learn about some simple sales techniques to enthuse your users. I will talk through different motivational strategies and how to get people motivated to use Salesforce. There are two main approaches to getting people on board. The first is the typical 'sales' methodology of looking at users' pain points and how you can solve them, and the second is a motivational strategy that aligns with the organisational culture. I would also recommend that you check out Chapter T on learning styles to give you a third element to your 'sales' strategy.

Motivating people to use Salesforce is a key ingredient of your change management and BA principles and it hinges on sales skills. When you introduce

Salesforce into a company, the staff need to buy into the CRM to result in good user adoption. Salesforce may have been sold to the executive sponsor, but how do you now sell it to the rest of the employees in the organisation? As a Salesforce consultant, your job is to sell Salesforce to stakeholders throughout the project life cycle, from BA to training, to get them engaged and excited about using it. If the word 'selling' makes you feel uncomfortable, you can reframe it as 'How do I make people happy by solving their pain points?' as ultimately that's what you're doing.

WHAT CAN GO WRONG?

The reality is, not everyone will understand what Salesforce can do for them, especially if they have never seen or heard about it before. The introduction of new technology can trigger different immediate reactions in your stakeholders. For some people it will be grief, anger, fear, denial, while for others it can be excitement and eagerness to learn.

If you have several stakeholders that are clearly unsure or reserved about Salesforce, which inevitably there will be, you need to move them to a place of excitement. Without a strategy to motivate people and get their buy-in, there will be low user adoption of the system. Signs to watch out for are people not showing up for workshops, managers not being engaged, people not preparing necessary information or speaking negatively in workshops.

HOW TO GET IT RIGHT

Where you have unenthusiastic users, you need to work your magic and turn this around by building a connection with people. You might need to do this through a one-to-one conversation with them as opposed to a group workshop in order to have a frank discussion.

To move people towards a place of excitement you need to elicit emotional motivations in them. In your BA process you will have uncovered how Salesforce CRM will help them to solve their problems, pain points or frustrations. These emotional motivators can be push factors, where people are trying to move away from pain, or they could be pull factors, where they want to experience a better version of the world.

Pain and solution narrative

You want to capture and present a 'pain and solution' narrative, and then re-emphasise this throughout all your communication in workshops and conversations during the whole of the project life cycle, to keep people enthused and engaged.

For example, when facilitating a workshop and presenting technical scenarios, you can re-emphasise the pain points but also propose the solution:

- 'If we introduce this automated email then it will reduce administration for you.'

- 'If we introduce a self-service portal it will help reduce customer frustration.'

Below I have listed some common examples of pain points that you might discover. Some of these should be evident to you from the business case document that has been compiled, but there can be multiple layers of pain points and what I would call a negative impact on teams and individuals. Don't be afraid to ask the deeper question: 'How does this issue impact you personally?' It's valuable to elicit the 'personal' issues beyond the business issues to really connect with your audience and get their buy-in.

For example, you might have a manager who isn't sleeping at night or can't switch off on holiday with their family as they don't have visibility about how their team is performing. Or someone who is working overtime at nights to compile data for reports for quarterly management meetings. Or a parent who isn't getting home on time due to the amount of admin they have to do.

It's recognising and solving these personal problems that helps to motivate people, more so than the business making more profit or reducing costs. As I have mentioned a few times, working as a Salesforce consultant is about making people happy.

Push factors	
Customer issues	Lack of information
	Customer frustration
	Disaggregated data
	Customer complaints
	Poor customer retention
Team frustration	Lack of data intelligence
	High employee turnover
	Disaggregated data
	Lack of co-ordination
	Poor performance
Pull factors	
Business improvement	Automated processes
	Reduce administration
	Improve employee retention
	Improve productivity
	Achieve quality standards
	Monitor operational and financial performance
	Structure for growth
Customer intelligence	Improve visibility
	Improve marketing
	Improve sales conversion
	Increase customer satisfaction

Deciding on the motivational strategies you will apply to engage people in Salesforce requires a considered approach based on:

- The business goals and motivations
- The organisational culture
- Individual factors
    - Personality types
    - Emotional states
    - Learning styles

Below is a mix of strategies for motivating people based on different emotional states. The approach you take will depend on what emotional state(s) the stakeholder is in and the organisational culture, so you will need to present these motivational strategies to the executive sponsor and/or CoE and ask them which they would prefer to adopt for their company and team members. Don't make this decision yourself.

At the end of this chapter, you should be able to embed softer sales techniques within your presentation style that will enable you to sell Salesforce to end users without you feeling like a hard-nosed salesperson. It's about discovering and then communicating how the product will benefit users, which ultimately makes you and your customers happier. If you utilise this narrative in your conversations, then selling the product will feel authentic for you.

Motivational Strategy	Reaction	Possible Interventions
Behavioural reward versus punishment	The culture is quite machine-oriented. People are used to being told what to do.	Recognition
		Gamification
		Financial bonus
		Career progression
	We assume individuals are motivated by rewards and will seek to avoid punishments.	Performance management
		Skills development
		Action learning
		Compliance
Cognitive positive reframing	There is an emotional reaction to change.	SMART goal setting
		Measures of success
		Visioning
	People are questioning the change.	NLP coaching
		Positive reframing of beliefs and attitudes
	They are experiencing limiting beliefs and feelings.	Action planning
		Self-esteem and confidence building
Psychodynamic emotional engagement	People are experiencing the grief cycle.	Counselling people
		Bringing to the surface hidden issues
	There are unconscious negative emotions bubbling up from experience.	Addressing emotions
		Facilitation and discussion
		Job security
		Honest conversations

(Continued)

(Cont)

Motivational Strategy	Reaction	Possible Interventions
Humanistic development and growth of the individual	They are interested to know what the change means for them. They want to know their choices for getting involved. They have lots of questions about it. They take responsibility for their situation. Individuals strive to achieve self-actualisation.[18]	Two-way communication channels. Learning and development. Addressing personal needs. Fostering consultation. Providing options. Encouraging self-responsibility. Addressing people's higher aspirations.

---

18 From Maslow's hierarchy of needs. See: A Maslow, *Motivation and Personality* (Harper & Row, 1970)

T
Training

The customer asks, 'How do I use Salesforce?'

As a consultant, do you know how to train users to maximise adoption?

In this chapter, we talk about what a Gold Star Training Strategy looks like. Training brings together all the BA and change management principles into one pot to create the final outcome. This is often the make-or-break point for adoption issues. Making sure you continue to sell Salesforce is key, as we covered in the last chapter, but in this chapter we'll look at how you reinforce this through tailoring how you deliver your content to appeal to people's different learning styles.

Delivering Salesforce training to end users isn't just about throwing together a training manual, delivering a three-hour training session and hoping for the best. That approach is likely to result in issues with low adoption.

Instead, to refine and work towards a perfect training strategy, you need to take into consideration:

- People's different learning styles
- People's different motivations
- Different training mediums and approaches

The success of a Salesforce implementation often lies in supporting people to engage with the process and system, rather than the technical skills involved in building the system.

WHAT CAN GO WRONG?

If you are delivering mentoring or training in just one type of learning style, it's likely that it won't meet the needs of some people. They just won't get it and will struggle to learn.

Additionally, if they don't know *why* they are learning Salesforce and what it means for them and their job, they won't be engaged. Explaining the business case as well as the personal motivational factors will start to grab their attention. We talked more about this in Chapter S.

HOW TO GET IT RIGHT

It's important to accommodate training into your budget, and to also appraise the value of training within the ROI. Often, budget can be limited, so make sure that the training budget is not squeezed to nothing as this is one of the most important areas of spend to achieve project success.

We need to approach training in a way that encompasses different learning styles to motivate people and deliver digestible content in the right way.

Learning styles and motivation

Learning styles can be understood using the VARK/VAK model, which I briefly mentioned earlier. Under this model, there are four learning styles: visual, auditory, read/write, kinaesthetic.

Can you identify your learning style? Quite often, we can be a combination, with a primary and secondary preference. Below is an example scenario that could help you work out your preferred learning style:

If you are putting together some DIY furniture, what do you like to do?

- Watch a video (auditory)
- Read the manual/instructions (read/write)
- Follow the pictures (visual)
- Just have a go without consulting anything (kinaesthetic)

You can also take a learning style test, and you could use this with people you are training to uncover their styles too. This is particularly valuable for one-to-one mentoring. In a group setting, you would want to try and appeal to all learning styles.

When you are motivating people to learn, you first need to ask yourself: why are they going to listen to this?

Typically, people with different learning styles need to be motivated in different ways and you should kick off any training agenda by addressing why they are there and learning ABC – this is to grab their attention. To reach everyone, you need to cover all the following aspects:

- **Visual** – they want to see what it's all about with a demo or taster video.
- **Auditory** – they want to know what is going to happen and when.
- **Read/write** – they need to know why they are doing this and what's in it for them, with facts/figures.
- **Kinaesthetic** – they want to get stuck in and hear and see examples of others using it.

To get this right and tick all of the above boxes, you'll need to think about how you are going to deliver the training content in a range of mediums. Below are some ideas:

- For read/write types, you need to prepare a training manual and Trailheads, as they prefer reading text.

- Visual types will prefer pictures, videos, live training sessions, slides.

- For auditory learners, you'll need live training, with verbal instruction and/or videos etc.

- For kinaesthetic learners, providing user scripts to run through will help them experience the content they're learning.

Access to training resources

Once you have delivered the training, you need to think about where the training resources are going to be kept so that people can continue to refer to them. You have a few options here.

The basic method, and a quick and easy solution, is to set up a shared external folder in a digital filing system. You could also use folders or Knowledge Articles in Salesforce, ideally with quick links embedded around the Salesforce system to navigate people back to the training resources.

Alternatively, you could introduce an LMS (learning management system). The benefit of an LMS is that you can upload content and set a training plan for your users in an ordered fashion. This will also provide an audit trail, showing you whether people have completed and watched the training material, meaning non-adopters can be flagged easily and a motivational strategy utilised.

You could use native in-situ training resources, setting up training tools that are already embedded in the Salesforce system and easy to find – think Trailhead Paths, My Trailhead, Learning Paths and In-App Guidance.

You could also consider third-party in-situ training and adoption tools. These enable you embed content, such as instructions and videos, around your Salesforce org to boost digital adoption within your user communities.

How to evaluate success

The success of a training strategy is indicated by the end-user adoption analytics. Are they as expected? Ask for feedback on the training and host a follow-up session for reflective learners in case they have any questions. The next chapter, on user adoption, will go into more detail on this.

We teach our trainees to communicate and deliver a holistic training strategy that will give the best chance of high user adoption, and to make full use of all their coaching tools and techniques.

For further reading on Salesforce training, Improved Apps have published some useful white papers on this subject. You can find these linked on the book resources page.

[QR code: SCAN ME]

- Delivering Zero classroom training
- Top ten tips for driving digital transformation, usage and adoption in the current climate
- Guide: How to get employee Salesforce onboarding right first time
- Guide: How to deliver Salesforce training that sticks
- Guide: 6 steps to successful just-in-time learning in Salesforce

At the end of this chapter, you should have a comprehensive understanding of how to create a holistic training strategy that can engage people with different learning styles and meets the needs of end users. You know to prioritise training in your allocation of time and budget, and how to measure its success by looking at user analytics.

PART SIX
EMBEDDING SALESFORCE

U
User Adoption

The customer asks, 'Is anyone actually using the Salesforce system?'

As a consultant, do you know how to assess and support good user adoption? Once you've delivered the training, how do you nurture and encourage user adoption? How do you assess adoption levels and troubleshoot risks?

In this chapter, find out how to create a user adoption strategy that will embed the Salesforce system for the long term.

WHAT CAN GO WRONG?

Without a user adoption strategy, you can find yourself in a scenario where you have delivered a great training session but six months later, no one is using the system. The result is a lot of time and money wasted. It can be difficult in this situation to relaunch and get everyone back on track to go live.

HOW TO GET IT RIGHT

> The senior management team needs to take on some of the responsibility for designing and implementing a user adoption strategy, so the consultant should facilitate a conversation around this to get it on the table and encourage those stakeholders to take ownership of it. As a Salesforce consultant, you can aid this process and make sure actions are taken to embed the system if you are moving on to a new project. Ultimately, it's about having an ongoing governance structure in place to support and assess user adoption.

The carrot/stick approach

When encouraging users to adopt the system, you can take a carrot or stick approach, or both. The carrot approach is the preferred approach, and if you have applied the BA and change management principles shared in this book then you will you be in the best place to apply and optimise this. But the stick approach should not be dismissed or overlooked, as it sets some clear business guidelines for users that are often needed. Both methods can and should be effectively applied where relevant.

The carrot approach

The carrot approach is about providing positive incentives and motivations to adopt the system. Some ways of applying this strategy are to:

- Realise the benefits that individuals requested from the system and communicate these during training.

- Generate reason(s) to login into system everyday – for example, to respond to new enquiries or cases that are no longer being routed by email.

- Utilise CRM team collaboration tools for stakeholder discussions.

- Introduce a gamification process. For example, if a deal is won, the system can send a celebration alert to the whole team, or give prizes to people earning the most Trailheads points.

- Create a reward system based on performance data that is captured within CRM reporting dashboards that are shown in team meetings.

- Celebrate success – identify the big wins and benefits of using the system and share these across the teams.

The stick approach

By contrast, the stick approach is less about incentives and more about setting an expectation, and/or suggesting negative consequences for not adopting the system. For example, you could:

- Create an official go-live date and time when everyone has to start using the system.

- Deliver continuous and targeted communication through a range of lean and rich communication methods and repeat these so that all intended users see and hear messages about the system go-live at least three times – often, people don't acknowledge a message until the third time they see it.

- Set out and maintain clear business rules within the training manual for use of CRM. For example, expectations around when calls or emails need to be logged, which fields of data need to be completed, when contacts should be added into the system. This level of detail is imperative when teaching someone how to use a CRM system.

- Rewrite job specifications and contracts to include requirements about when and how they need to use the CRM as part of their job. Then, if they don't input information into the CRM, or refuse to use it, you can go down a performance management route to ensure adoption.

- Utilise the CRM dashboards for performance management in team meetings and one-to-ones to showcase team performance. Champion the Salesforce Ohana mantra of, 'If it's not in Salesforce, it doesn't exist.'

- Align reviews or bonus payments to performance information captured within the CRM to keep people focused on what they need to do to achieve their goals.

Key pillars for embedding the system

In my experience, there are five key pillars for embedding a Salesforce CRM system: having a support team in place, institutionalising change as the norm, establishing a change culture within the organisation, establishing quality control and evaluating the success of the project. Below are some of the actions you can take within each of these pillars.

Having a support team in place

- Look at ways to embed on-demand training resources within your system so it is easily accessible to users. You can use the tools that we mentioned in Chapter T to embed training content that can give real-time support to users to navigate and use the system.

- Provide an ongoing support service to ensure the team have easy access to answers, advice or coaching as required.

- Set up a CRM support desk so users can raise cases for issues, training requests or any ideas they have.

- During the first six months after go-live, set up regular working groups with users to invite verbal feedback from people so that you unearth any hidden dramas that might be arising.

- Share learning and any updates with the team to embed a continual improvement process.

- Produce resources that can be shared and accessed as required by the team.

Institutionalising change as the norm

- Establish new expectations of managers, staff or stakeholders as the norm.

- Redesign job roles and partner contracts etc.

- Establish new KPIs and performance management frameworks.

Establishing a change culture in the organisation

- Foster an environment of continual change to improve quality and maximise opportunities.

- Maintain a champions team and ongoing feedback loop from users to continue an evolution pathway for new and existing changes.

- Refine and embed the change management process for the future.

Establishing quality control

- Monitor whether the new approach is being adopted by the relevant teams and address any resistance as necessary.

- Maintain communication with users to solve issues, counter resistance or solve problems that are affecting use or outcome quality.

- Continue to refine and develop the solution based on feedback to ensure it meets requirements.

Evaluating the success of the project

- Evaluate the effectiveness of the change management process amongst different stakeholders.

- Collect and review feedback from users to see if the solution is meeting their expectations.

- Undertake a cost–benefit analysis to review whether the solution has produced the anticipated benefits.

How to assess adoption

You can assess the level of adoption by identifying metrics that indicate improved productivity and engagement. But what to measure?

In light of tighter purchasing budgets, it is imperative to prove not only the ROI of technology purchases through usage, but also increased productivity and engagement improvements through the use of Digital Adoption Solutions (DAS). To achieve this, application leaders/product owners must work to support the business units in creating a set of metrics that can be tracked.

Most often, these can also be correlated to money saved or improved revenue outcomes. Some examples of metrics you can use, ways of measuring them and outcomes they're linked to, are provided below.

Number of support tickets resolved and time spent resolving tickets

Measurement:

- Number of 'how do I' tickets by application
- Length of time taken to resolve issue

Outcome:

- Fewer tickets allow for more complex problem resolution and increased end-user satisfaction (higher engagement)
- Reduced length of resolve time allows N percent group overall response time improvement

Training time

Measurement:

- Reduced hours spent on onboarding and change management

Outcome:

- Decrease in training costs due to in-application learning
- Artefacts created by DAS do not need to be created by the training department
- Change management training may be eliminated
- Training reinforcement leads to greater end-user satisfaction (higher productivity)

Onboarding time to productivity

Measurement:

- Time from hire to fully productive

Outcome:

- Reduced onboard time saves money and increases contribution rate for employee (eg, less time to get a seller productive and delivering revenue)

Data quality issues

Measurement:

- Data validation

Outcome:

- Reduced data issues
- Increased data completeness

Employee satisfaction

Measurement:

- Employee engagement survey scores, NPS score or similar satisfaction scores

Outcome:

- Increased satisfaction leads to higher engagement and productivity
- Correlation to customer satisfaction

There are some more useful white papers on this topic by Improved Apps, available on the book resources page.

- Guide: The three roadblocks to Salesforce adoption
- Guide: How to find out why people aren't using Salesforce

There is also a website (www.digitaladoption.info) offering a free learning platform for digital adoption and knowledge management, where you can access a plethora of information to aid in selecting the ideal digital adoption vendor for your business and ensure you leave no stone unturned.

Your final adoption strategy checklist

Overall, your final user adoption plan and strategy will have three key components. Work your way through the checklist below and you'll be primed for high user adoption rates and a successful project launch.

1. Strategy

- Do you have a carrot and stick approach to encourage user adoption?
- Are all of the relevant team managers on board with adoption?
- What KPIs have been defined that can clarify good user adoption and have these been incorporated within job descriptions?
- Have Salesforce champions been identified and trained for each team?

2. Ongoing support

- Are Salesforce champions ready and prepared to support users daily?
- Has a process been established for users to raise issues, ask questions and request updates?
- Has a training programme been designed and rolled out?
- If ongoing changes are requested, do you know how these will be prioritised and set out?
- If ongoing improvements and changes are made to the system, do you have a clear way for this to be communicated back to users?
- Do you have training resources embedded into the system?

3. Monitoring

- Have you set up real-time analytics to review user adoption?
- Where are the main user adoption issues arising? For example, are they related to data, the user interface etc? Can you categorise and troubleshoot issues?
- Has an ongoing process been established to oversee data quality management?

USER ADOPTION

At the end of this chapter, you have a long list of things to include in a user adoption strategy that will support the ongoing success of your CRM post-implementation. This area is often overlooked when a consultant exits the building post-implementation, but it's important that someone is left holding the baby and nurturing it during those early days when it's a new thing in everyone's world. This requires constant attention, assessment and appraisal to ensure that everything is moving in the right direction to achieve the desired results.

Thank you to Improved Apps, the only Salesforce security-reviewed digital adoption partner, for sponsoring this chapter. Improved Apps are passionate about educating Salesforce professionals about digital adoption and can help you embed your content in context to boost digital adoption within your user communities. Their free Improved Usage Tracker tool gives insights, data and dashboards to show you exactly how your users are engaging with Salesforce, enabling you to identify the potential for efficiencies and boost productivity for greater Salesforce ROI.

V
Value Assessment

> The customer asks, 'What value is the CRM giving to the organisation?'
>
> *As a consultant, do you know how to assess what value the CRM is creating for the business?*

This chapter marks the beginning of the end of this book, where we move on from what could go wrong and how to do things right to instead focus on next steps and reflections. In this chapter, we find out how to evaluate the success of a completed project and communicate your trailblazer success story.

Earlier in the book, we talked about the KPIs for ROI and the business case for a CRM. At some stage after the go-live date you will need to revisit these with the client to assess whether the expected business benefits of the project have materialised for the client.

How quickly you can see and assess the benefits will be dependent on the project and the deliverables, but normally you would be in a position to assess value six months to one year after the go-live date. Depending on your relationship with the customer, you might do this value appraisal yourself or it might be led by an internal team of stakeholders. Normally, it would involve a mixture of elicitation techniques including direct conversations with managers, a review of tangible metrics and a questionnaire with end users. Ideally, the outcome would be a body of quantitative and qualitative evidence to show improvements against the original KPIs and business case that were proposed for the project.

In addition, as a consultant, you want to be able to tell a 'trailblazer' story of the Salesforce project, with a great case study that you can add to your CV.

Here are some examples of the typical stories you would want to elicit and capture to demonstrate success:

- A non-profit was struggling to hit its donor fundraising targets as it had no online payment facility and could only take cheques or cash. By introducing NPSP and an integrated online payment solution, it has increased its donor fundraising revenue by 100% within one year.

- An organisation had a low repeat sales rate for existing customers as they were not adding them to a subscriber list for ongoing communication.

With the introduction of Salesforce and an e-marketing solution, they now send regular communications out to their customers, and they have tripled sales from existing customers within a year.

- A customer support team were struggling to deal with the volume of cases they were receiving and response times were sometimes beyond forty-eight hours. With the introduction of Salesforce and Experience Cloud they were able to provide a self-service hub for customers to find answers to their questions. This reduced the number of cases that got raised by half, and response times to existing cases is now within twenty-four hours.

- A finance team were having to replicate sales income into the financial system, creating duplicate work. By integrating Sales Cloud with financial accounting software, the finance team has halved the amount spent on bookkeeping support each month due to the time saved.

If the Salesforce project hasn't yet realised its business objectives, go back to Chapter L and uncover the root cause using the NLP Logical Levels to try and resolve the issue and get the project back on track to success.

At the end of this chapter, you should know how to demonstrate the tangible value of Salesforce and of your role, enabling you to boost your confidence, salary and job security.

W
Wrapping Up

> The customer asks, 'Who is left holding the baby when the consultant goes?'
>
> *As a consultant, are you confident that the management team know how to manage the new Salesforce CRM going forward?*

When your role as the Salesforce consultant comes to an end, you need to empower your client to manage the system beyond your involvement. In this chapter, find out how to offboard a customer and wrap up a project successfully.

Some of the core elements here tie in with previous chapters:

- Governance – make sure there is a good governance structure in place and management buy-in is strong.

- Hiring a team – help the organisation ensure they have the right internal team in place to manage the system and users in the long term.

- Identify and train champions – check that the organisation has champions in place to support users.

- An awesome admin – educate the Salesforce admin on their roles and responsibilities.

- Training – leave the organisation with training resources that are easily accessible for end users and that can be edited as needed by the in-house Salesforce team to accommodate future updates.

- User adoption – help the organisation to roll out a user adoption strategy that is owned by management and will ensure user adoption is continually assessed.

If you are an external Salesforce consultant and are leaving a new Salesforce admin in-situ to manage the system, it is a good idea to educate them on where they can access help and training to support them in their role. You should also introduce them to general resources within the Salesforce Ohana.

Below are some of the things I would recommend you include in the training resources you provide:

- **Salesforce training.** Give the internal staff directions of where and how to access Salesforce training if they need it. For example, you could direct them to the Supermums Training Admin, Consultancy Skills and Marketing Cloud training courses: https://supermums.org/training

- **Salesforce help site:** https://help.salesforce.com/home. This is a great place to do a quick search of general help info. A Google search should bring up this content too, but it can also be found by clicking on 'Help and Training' from within Salesforce.

- **Success community:** https://success.salesforce.com. This is where users/Salesforce staff collaborate on answering questions and sharing ideas. It's an online forum that can provide fast responses (often from other users), but it's also worth browsing previously asked questions as someone may have asked a question before.

- **Salesforce support:** https://help.salesforce.com/HTUnauthContactSupport. This is where you can contact Salesforce support directly and log a case. If the organisation or in-house admin needs additional personalised support and training, there is a paid-for Premier Support service.

- **Salesforce Trailhead:** https://trailhead.salesforce.com. A complete interactive guide to Salesforce learning. Trailhead is a great way to learn about Salesforce. As the Salesforce consultant, you can devise some trails for your client to give them focus and direction on the platform.

- **Salesforce Ohana user groups:** https://trailhead.salesforce.com/trailblazer-community/groups. A place to connect and engage with other Salesforce admins locally or who share similar passions, attend events to learn new things and discuss challenges with peers.

- **Trust site:** http://trust.salesforce.com. This site reports on the status of the Salesforce system if there are any outages and the admin needs to troubleshoot.

In this chapter, you have a handy checklist for off-boarding a client and resources you can provide to leave them empowered to manage their system beyond your engagement.

PART SEVEN
BECOMING A SUPER CONSULTANT

X
X-Ray Of The Project

> After the project is complete, you can ask yourself, 'How did you perform on the Salesforce project?'
>
> *As a consultant, do you know how to evaluate your project and leadership?*

Doing an X-ray of a Salesforce project is a great way to assess how a project performed against the principles set out in this book. You can do this independently but also with the project team.

When you do this exercise, be kind to yourself and make sure you put everything in context. A project will rarely run perfectly, so be prepared to weather the storms that come your way and know that there is always a sun shining on the other side. With every project, you and your team members will be going on an emotional journey; there are various frameworks that can help you get to grips with this and may be useful at various stages:

- The **Tuckman Team Development Model** can be useful for learning how to work with a new team of people.
- The **Learning Life Cycle** is helpful to understand, both for yourself and your users, as everyone grapples with learning something new.
- **Kübler-Ross's five-stage Grief Cycle** is handy to refer to when challenges and blockers arise on the project.
- The **Growth Versus Fixed Mindset Confrontation** is relevant when imposter syndrome rears its head.

It's important that you be mindful of the emotions that can arise, realise that they are normal and that any difficulties can be overcome when they are understood and tackled the right way.

With this awareness in mind, review the variables below objectively to reflect on the strengths and challenges of the project process:

- What went well, and what didn't?
- What could you control, and what couldn't you?
- What would you do differently next time and improve upon?

- What training and skills development do you need to pursue in order to do things better next time?

In addition, consider whether you experienced any of the following:

Challenges	Stage	Strengths
Insufficient time and budget	Design	Management buy-in
Inadequate preparation		Full user consultation
Lack of internal ownership over processes and KPIs		Clear business case
		Clear objectives
		Internal CRM resources
No change management strategy		Technical knowledge
Lack of technical understanding		In-depth BA
Insufficient user testing	Build	Agile PM
Poor Agile PM		Iterative design and development
No PM		
No internal facilitator		User testing and feedback loop
		Management engagement
Insufficient training	Training	Management buy-in and ownership
Unengaged managers		
No time for productivity lag		Updated process maps and manual
Poor resources		In-house champions(s)
		Investment in training

(Continued)

(Cont)

Challenges	Stage	Strengths
Unclear business rules	Adoption	Data integrity management
No internal champion		
Poor maintenance		Business rules followed
Poor data quality		
		Ongoing maintenance
		CRM as the norm

Next, you can re-assess your personal level of confidence in running a Salesforce project by taking our Salesforce Consultancy Skills Quiz on the book resources page and seeing how far you've come since opening this book.

How did it go? At the end of this chapter, you should be able to identify and celebrate your wins and take steps to resolve any issues.

Y
Your Career Plan

> Looking to the future, you think, 'What Salesforce project should I do next?'
>
> *As a consultant, do you know how to get a promotion and accelerate your career?*

If you start out on the lower salary ranges as a Salesforce admin, it is possible to double your salary as a Salesforce professional and progress up the ranks if you keep pursuing your goals. In this chapter, I set out some of the things you can do that will make a real difference to your earning potential, giving you a clear roadmap for doubling your Salesforce salary.

To be upfront: you aren't going to double your salary overnight. How long it takes will depend on you – your time, your commitment and your transferrable skills. There are some moves that will be quicker than others.

To put this goal into context, it will involve upskilling and progression from one job role to another with incremental salary increases in between. Typically, you can negotiate pay increments every year if you have added value to your CV in the ways mentioned below. In terms of setting your overall career goals, here are five of the career paths you can decide to pursue to double your salary potential within three years in the Salesforce ecosystem:

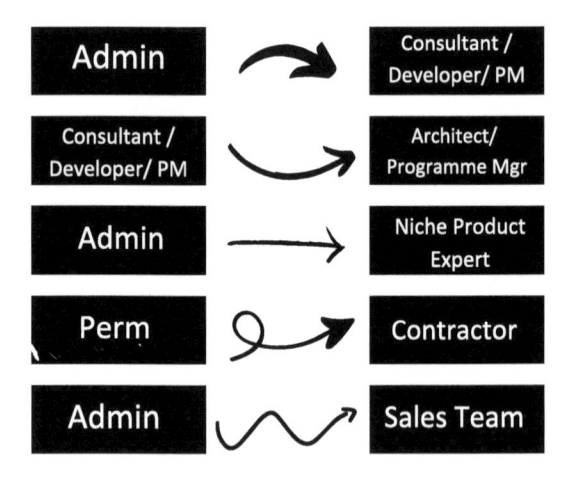

Admin	Consultant / Developer / PM
Consultant / Developer / PM	Architect / Programme Mgr
Admin	Niche Product Expert
Perm	Contractor
Admin	Sales Team

1. If you are progressing from a junior Salesforce admin to a consultant/developer/project manager/product owner, this could take three years.

2. If you are progressing from a business analysis/Salesforce consultant/developer to a CRM programme manager/architect role, this could take three years.

3. You could move from a permanent role to a contractor and double your salary within a month, as the day rates are higher, but bear in mind you will then be responsible for holiday pay, sick pay and training, so you will need to weigh up the benefits against these costs.

4. You could go from being a Salesforce admin to a niche product expert within a year – think MuleSoft, Marketing Cloud, CPQ, Vlocity, FSL products. In these niches, there is a shortage of expertise and high demand for talent, so salaries are higher.

5. You could go from being a Salesforce admin/consultant into a sales or solution engineering role within three months and double your salary by earning commission. If you love getting people excited about technology by discussing their challenges, proposing solutions and building out solutions as demos, then this is a great role to look at.

Keen to double your salary? Complete the exercise below to create a plan of action.

REFLECTIVE EXERCISE

Below is a list of things you can do to shift the dial on your salary. Grab a notebook and write down what you can do right now, and start creating your vision for the future.

Here are ten ways to add value to your résumé and salary.

1. Change roles every couple of years

This didn't used to be the norm, and I can almost hear you gasping at how unprofessional it sounds, but suspend your judgement for a moment. Every time you change jobs, it's an opportunity to progress your career and earning potential. This can be within the same company or in another company. Everyone should have the ability to reach their potential. The best way to do this is to move with the intention of building your experience. Try out working for different types and sizes of organisation to get wide-ranging exposure to diverse products, cultures and approaches. For example, you could work for a Salesforce consultancy, independent software vendor (ISV) or end customer, ranging from small businesses to enterprises. They could be global to local or non-profit, commercial or public sector entities. All of these aspects will influence what salary they offer and the level of responsibility you have.

Two years is the average time to change roles in the Salesforce ecosystem because people are thirsty to get project and product experience and to keep learning new things. There's no guarantee you will get that by staying in one business. Take advantage of opportunities that come your way, stop trying to be perfect and be brave in putting yourself forward for bigger, better opportunities even if you don't feel ready. As a Salesforce professional, you have an unquenchable thirst for learning and you like solving problems. It's in your DNA to feel comfortable being uncomfortable, so push yourself out of your comfort zone. You might be surprised at what's possible and your pay packet and superannuation will reward you for it.

2. Apply for a role two or three levels above your current pay grade

Just because a company has transparent salary banding and pay grades, this doesn't mean you can't skip a few levels, especially if you have the required experience and expertise and are able to communicate this clearly. This is a tactic that I've seen work well over and over again in both large and small organisations. The trick is to focus on building a business case to demonstrate the value you can add – this might not be obvious from what you're doing in your current role.

It's nobody's business what you currently earn. That question that recruiters often ask – 'How much are you currently on?' – only perpetuates the gender salary gap. Reply by asking them what the role is paying instead. Don't let what you currently earn get in the way of what you should and could be earning.

3. Conduct a benchmarking activity

Find out if you're being paid at the same level as your peers. Asking for a role to be benchmarked is a great way to find out where you sit on the scale within (and outside of) your organisation and may result in a sizeable adjustment in your favour. Also check out the various Salesforce surveys, find similar job specs and ask for a salary survey internally to share visibly if there is a gender pay gap issue.

4. Get more consultancy skills

Regardless of the Salesforce role you apply for, boosting your CV with consultancy skills will give you a better chance of doing a great job as well as earning more. Typically, business analysts earn 10k more than admins, and project managers can earn up to £20k more. As a consultant, solo admin, product owner or project manager you will be expected to have all of these skills alongside the technical experience. Revisit the consultancy skills chapter in the book if you need to.

5. Add DevOps certifications to your knowledge

DevOps is now being mentioned in most of the technical job specifications from admin to architect and everything in between. It's highly recommended that you learn and master the principles of DevOps, one of the DevOps platforms and add this to your skill set and CV. This will contribute to your earning potential. Revisit Chapter D to explore this avenue.

6. Obtain five more Salesforce certifications

To advance between the different job roles, you are typically looking at earning five certifications for each move, to progress your knowledge and expertise. The product knowledge that comes with five certifications will advance your salary by between £10–20k.

As an admin, you would take a combination of Admin, App Builder, Advanced, Platform 1 and Product Cloud certs to double your salary by becoming a Salesforce consultant/junior developer. From a consultant/developer role you would complete a combination of Product Cloud and Architect certifications to progress towards an architect role and double your salary. For specialist roles, such as in Marketing Cloud, you would earn the relevant credentials related to the products.

7. Sell your professional experience

Apply for roles where you can transfer your industry experience, management experience or product knowledge. Build up and present your portfolio of projects and expertise to position yourself as an expert. Demonstrate the ROI, especially in terms of the financial improvements that projects have provided for your customers – revisit Chapter K on how to measure ROI in the book. The more knowledge and experience you can share, the higher the salary you can leverage.

8. Don't shy away from management roles

Women are less represented in management roles, so companies are trying to balance out their gender split by hiring more women into these roles. Quite often, being a manager doesn't mean more responsibility, though you must learn the art of building a great team, delegating tasks and planning your time. By taking on a management and/or leadership role you can increase your salary, progress your career and focus on building and supporting a high-performing team to flourish below you through coaching and mentoring. To support yourself, invest in a great coach and mentor who can help you to stay accountable and in check – revisit Chapter F if you need to.

9. Build your personal brand

Companies will be attracted to candidates who have a good reputation and profile in the Salesforce Ohana, as this shows goodwill and is also good for their own brand and customer experience. What can you do to share your knowledge with others in the Salesforce Ohana? You could write blogs, create videos, speak at events or produce a podcast. It's fantastic to see what other trailblazers have created. If you love sharing and helping others, then build a personal brand – this will inevitably lead to being able to command a higher salary, too. Turn to Chapter Z for ideas on how to build your personal brand.

10. Become a third-party app expert

Get to understand a suite of commonly used third-party apps to improve your management and use of Salesforce and demonstrate the value they can bring to a solution. Quite often, people only learn to use third-party apps as the need arises, but there are many apps out there that we should be proactively using to enhance the way we manage Salesforce products and create solutions. Demonstrating your experience and knowledge of third-party apps, particularly ones that a potential client/employer is using, will definitely increase your earning potential.

Z
Zone Of Genius

> Ask yourself, 'What am I really good at?'
>
> *As a consultant, do you know what your zone of genius is and how to maximise it?*

One way to advance your career and build your confidence, land a job or get a promotion is to carve out a niche in the Salesforce arena. The first step to achieving this is to understand what you are passionate about – what makes you shine when you talk about it?

Some ideas of where your niche might be are:

- Industry-related – Salesforce focuses on selling its product into certain industry verticals. Do you have relevant experience in a specific industry? If so, you could focus on this as your niche.

- Product-related – do you have a passion for a particular Salesforce product that you could become an expert in? Do you want to immerse yourself in that product and all of the third-party extensions, be it Service Cloud, Sales Cloud, Marketing Cloud, CPQ, MuleSoft or anything else?

- Skill-related – are you particularly great at, for example, admin, automation, BA, project management, DevOps, training, coding or architecture? You could position yourself as a specialist in one of these skills and share your top tips.

- Mission-related – do you want to champion and support certain members of the community from a similar background – for example, equality and/or diversity groups, a particular locality, or industry customers? This is what I did by launching Supermums.

Once you've identified your niche, you should focus on building your confidence in this area to feel like you have the authority to speak as an expert. Seek feedback and testimonials from people you have worked with and post these on LinkedIn, so they are publicly available for people to see. Accept and appreciate great feedback, let it boost your confidence and belief in yourself.

Some other ways to build your confidence and gain traction in your niche are to:

- Complete any relevant certifications that back up your expertise
- Start to document your winning formula, strategy or tips that you would share with others
- Mentor others who are entering this area
- Start presenting on this topic within internal meetings or training sessions
- Share some of your top tips on social media

Once you feel comfortable with and confident in your niche and believe that you have something valuable to offer, it's time to step it up. Put together a one-page profile that summarises your speaking topics, your background, testimonials and your credentials and use this to leverage new opportunities.

Some ideas of ways to amplify your personal brand are to:

- Apply for a role or ask to become the internal specialist/head of department in your niche
- Put yourself forward to speak at user group events
- Offer to co-host a user group
- Submit speaker sessions for Salesforce community events
- Write articles to submit to existing blogs

- Start your own blog and post regularly
- Put yourself forward as a guest speaker on a podcast
- Start your own podcast
- Launch a YouTube channel and create video tutorials

Find the medium that suits you and the one you are most comfortable working within. Seek training on how to present well or how to optimise a blog or YouTube channel if you decide to launch a platform on your own. It's time to step out of your comfort zone, but you don't have to do it alone. Surround yourself with experts who can help you on your way. Most importantly, enjoy it and shine. Find and focus on your zone of genius and become a Super Salesforce Consultant.

Be sure to tell me how you are getting on, what you are doing and look me up on LinkedIn so we can celebrate your success. I can't wait to see what you achieve, so go blaze your trail.

Conclusion

After running through all of the different components of leading a successful Salesforce CRM project, you should now feel reassured rather than overwhelmed by the prospect. Everyone reading this book will be on their own journey of learning and at a different stage in their Salesforce career, so don't worry if you aren't implementing everything just yet. The important thing is that you are leaning in and learning how to do things, or checking that what you are doing is right. That makes you amazing. This capacity to appraise, renew and reshape how you deliver something if you feel it needs a new or better approach will make you a fantastic Salesforce consultant.

Whatever stage you're at, this book should have answered a lot of questions for you, and possibly raised some for you to ask yourself. I hope it has helped you to appraise your current level of knowledge and that you can start formulating a strategy for leading your Salesforce projects in a confident way.

You can use the book and the online resources I've linked to as a trusty checklist and toolkit to dip into as and when you need when working through a project. Plus, you can carve out a plan for your career to ignite your motivation. What experience do you want to gain? What skills do you want to develop? Which areas do you want to specialise in? If you can lead projects with confidence then the world is your oyster and there should be nothing stopping you from ramping up your salary and accelerating your career progression.

If you would like to share any lightbulb moments or benefits you feel the book has given you, please do leave a review and/or share it with anyone you feel might enjoy it. I would love to hear your thoughts.

If you think you might want further support to advance your skills and confidence in leading a Salesforce project, there are two ways that I, and Supermums, can support you going forward. First, you can sign up to the Supermums Consultancy Skills Course content, which offers you further in-depth training and mentoring on business analysis, change management and Agile PM, as well as more intensive BA information for different Salesforce projects and areas covered in this book. At Supermums we can also support companies to hire emerging and experienced Salesforce talent and upskill individuals with Salesforce skills, so let us know if we can help in any way.

Second, you could hire me as a strategic adviser to support the Salesforce team, the executive sponsor and CoE team within your organisation to help them understand how to lead a Salesforce project with confidence. I do this through delivering coaching and training on the core principles and areas covered within this book.

Acknowledgements

I would like to extend my gratitude to the sponsors who support Supermums and, in some cases, have also contributed to the contents of this book.

- Slalom
- Improved Apps
- DESelect
- Provar
- MarCloud
- Hubbl

BECOME A SUPER SALESFORCE CONSULTANT

- Gearset
- GridMate
- SharinPix
- Validity
- 360SMS

Introducing Supermums

Supermums helps people to launch and accelerate their Salesforce career in three main ways:

- Free educational events – Supermums runs a series of events throughout the year, which can include peer certification study groups, ISV demo jams and experience weeks.

- Training courses – Supermums is a Salesforce authorised training provider. We deliver flexible public and in-house admin, Marketing Cloud and consultancy skills training courses with certified instructors across EMEA and USA time zones.

- Talent supply and recruitment services – Supermums can supply emerging and experienced talent to fill a range of permanent or contract roles to help implement or manage Salesforce.

The above services are open to everyone. Proceeds from the sale of this book will be reinvested into a bursary fund to offer free or discounted training places to women who have suffered from domestic violence and want to regain their financial independence.

As a social enterprise, we are passionate about our mission of supporting mothers and tackling the following agendas: reducing the gender pay gap; supporting women returners; increasing the number of women in tech; and addressing the digital skills gap.

Companies and people can support our mission through hiring our talent, sponsoring our educational content (including this book) and volunteering as ambassadors, mentors and trainers. We currently have over 180 volunteers worldwide that support us.

The Supermums Consultancy Skills course fully equips you to further your Salesforce career. Over twelve weeks, it provides live weekly masterclasses and on-demand training in BA, Agile PM, change management and DevOps, with expert mentoring from Heather.

If you want to learn more about the Supermums Consultancy Skills course, scan below:

The Author

Heather Black started out as an accidental admin and then upskilled to become a freelance Salesforce consultant in 2011. She is eight-times certified, a change management and NLP practitioner and holds both a diploma in business analysis practice and a foundation in Agile DSDM project management.

Heather ran a Salesforce consultancy for ten years, winning the EMEA Salesforce Consulting Partner of the Year award. During this time, she oversaw over 700 projects with 350 customers and was a member of the Salesforce EMEA Partner Advisory Board.

Since 2020, she has focused on training and advising executive sponsors and Salesforce professionals on how to lead digital transformation and Salesforce projects, by teaching them essential skills via the Supermums Consultancy Skills course and a Level 4 Business Analysis Qualification, while also providing one-to-one mentoring.

She is the founder of Supermums, a global social enterprise that helps to launch and accelerate the careers of women within the Salesforce ecosystem through providing a training and recruitment service. Since 2016, Supermums has supported over 1,000 trainees and more than 200 employers to find super talent.

Heather is a coveted Golden Hoodie winner, due to her efforts championing women in tech, and was recognised in the 100 Most Influential Women in Tech by *Computer Weekly* and in the Tech Women 100 Awards by *We Are Tech Women*, amongst other accolades.

She writes content and speaks regularly at Salesforce events and user groups on topics related to the A to Z of how to lead a Salesforce project, how to be a super Salesforce consultant and how to accelerate your career as a woman in tech with the ambitious women mindset. She has presented for audiences of over 10,000 including at Dreamforce, Salesforce World Tour London, Salesforce World Tour Manchester, Dreamforce to You London, Marie Claire and Salesforce Partner Events, MERC and Chase 25.

INTRODUCING SUPERMUMS

- 🌐 www.supermums.org
- ❲f❳ www.facebook.com/supermumsglobal/
- ❲in❳ www.linkedin.com/company/supermumsglobal/
- 🐦 https://twitter.com/SupermumsGlobal
- 📷 www.instagram.com/supermumsglobal/